ULTIMATE
LEADERSHIP

10 RULES FOR SUCCESS

Chris Cebollero

Ultimate Leadership:
10 Rules for Success

by Chris Cebollero

ISBN-13: 978-1530745685
ISBN-10:1530745683

Acknowledgements

For my Family. Without your unflagging support, I wouldn't have accomplished so many of my life-long dreams.

I'd like to also offer special thanks to all of the people in my life, past, present and future who have taken the time to honor me with their knowledge and support.

Because of you, I believe strongly in the power of building people up and giving back to the next generation. This book is just a small part of my commitment to build the next generation of leaders.

For all of you readers, my wish for you is that you use this book as a tool to become the best leader that you can! I know that you will grow and learn, and maybe even fail sometimes, but that's how we learn. When you are ready, find a mentor to continue helping you grow into your leadership ability and never stop learning and growing.

This is just the beginning.

—Chris Cebollero

Advanced Praise

"Chris's 10 Rules for Success are a Philosophy that works. Having been part of his leadership team for a number of years, I've seen this practice transform our organization. If you follow these 10 Rules, you will see success! Guaranteed."

—Tricia P. O'Laughlin

"This resource will solidify rules and skills needed to develop a highly engaged team of professionals. Based on close to 30 years of experience, Ultimate Leadership: 10 Rules for Success shares the insight we needed as leaders from the very beginning of our careers."

—Jennifer Cordia,
VP Patient Care Services/Chief Nursing Officer

"Ultimate Leadership: 10 Rules for Success is a must have resource for Business Leaders! Chris uses his 30 years of "real in the trenches" leadership experience to ensure the development of a strong, successful and profitable organization using his 10 Leadership rules. There is no myth or theory here."

—TC Bradley,
Chairman and Founder, New Life Vision, LLC

Table of Contents

INTRODUCTION

The pinnacle of my leadership career occurred during the summer of 2014. On this particular Saturday, it started off like any normal Saturday, mowing the lawn, washing my 100 pound Akita "Grace," which was always a task in itself, and preparing to barbeque some steaks for lunch. Just about that time, the phone rings and my second in charge is on the line. He told me we had a situation at work. After that call, I made the decision to forgo my plans for grilling and head to the office.

My career for the past 30 years was in the medical field. I specialized as a Paramedic and worked in some very busy EMS systems across the United States. My current tenure was Chief of Emergency Medical Services for Christian Hospital, a role I had for 4 years at this point. Little did I know that once I arrived on scene to assess the situation, my leadership skills were going to be tested to their maximum limit.

On this day in August, a white police officer shot an unarmed African American teen named Mike Brown, and the city of Ferguson, MO was getting ready to be thrust into the international spotlight for rioting, looting and assaults. I arrived on scene approximately three hours after the shooting, and our ambulances were in an area about a mile away from where the shooting took place at the Canfield Apartments. The Canfield Apartments were already a powder keg ready to explode. For our safety, police asked us to leave and find a safer place to "stage" and wait for further instructions.

Mike Brown's body lay in the middle of the road on this hot August day for more than 4 hours, and the protests grew louder, more heated, and eventually aggressive. Once I arrived at the staging area, my needle of concern for employee safety was immediately pegged in the red. Even though we moved to a so called "safe area," there were more than 300 yelling and screaming protesters with signs that read, "Kill the police," "Stop murdering our kids" and "The police just murdered my son." Along with the protesters, there were also regional and local SWAT teams with armored vehicles, and three news cameras that were trying to capture the emotion of the event.

As I approached my workforce already on scene, there were some quick logistical decisions that had to be made, then came the need for some situational and crisis awareness with my team. My brain was moving in 1000 different directions; the flood of information I was trying to process was overwhelming. It was at this time I noticed that my workforce was looking to me for directions, answers and truthfully, some comfort. This is where this nightmare began for me, and whatever happened from this point forward, I needed to make certain the decisions made were based on all my experiences, successes and knowledge as a leader.

For the next 19 days in August, and then the months leading up to the November Grand Jury announcement, as a team and an organization, our leadership was tested to the extreme. What worked yesterday, would not work today. The process developed for caring for patients had to be reworked, we had to monitor social media, we needed body armor, we needed some additional training and we needed a pipeline into some reliable communication and coordination.

I can share with you now that this was a scary, stressful time and there were many times I questioned the decisions I needed to make to ensure the safety of my workforce and leadership team. At the end of this event, none of our folks were hurt, everyone went home safely and we were recognized for an outstanding job well done. As a leader, I could not be more proud of my workforce and my leadership team. Everyone was professional and dedicated to giving the best patient care, despite the circumstances. This was truly the crown jewel in my leadership experience, and everything I had experienced up until this point prepared me for this very moment in time.

Even though the decisions I made during the Ferguson crisis assisted in keeping everyone safe and allowed us to remain professional during a stressful event, I can share with you that my leadership skills were not always as tight as they could have been. To be honest, it was quite the opposite for a long time.

Welcome to **Ultimate Leadership: 10 Rules for Leadership Success**. These 10 rules were created out of my successes, achievements, mistakes and failures. These were hard-won lessons I learned on my journey to becoming a successful leader.

My leadership journey began as a leader in the U.S. Air Force in 1986. I was unprepared and lacked the needed experience to lead the workforce with success. I have to admit to you that this very first leadership position was a failure for me and my employees. In part, it was due to not having a mentor or someone to teach me how to *be* a good leader. I was growing my leadership career on a foundation of failure. My experiences with this kind of failure led me to learn valuable lessons the hard way, for the next 10 years!

In the beginning, my leadership style was based on egotism, ignorance, and wanting to advance my career instead of growing my team. Over this timeframe, mistakes mounted and lessons were learned. Leadership is both an art and a science, and if you do not know the science of leadership, you will not be able to paint the portrait of success.

My leadership journey eventually allowed me to learn the necessary science that allowed me to develop an award-winning organization and be recognized as an international leader.

Follow each of these 10 rules and you will increase your leadership effectiveness, enjoy a positive reputation, and have an organization whose workforce is engaged with a high level of employee satisfaction.

Thank you for allowing me to join you on your leadership journey. If you are interested in purchasing a license to teach Ultimate Leadership: 10 Rules for Success, please visit www.chriscebollero.com.

—*Chris Cebollero*

Chris Cebollero is an internationally recognized leader, author and motivational speaker. Chris spent 30 years in the medical field where he led hundreds of medical professionals. He has a proven track record of developing the next generation of leaders.

In 2014, his experience served him and his Emergency Medical Service teams well as they were thrust right in the middle of the riots, looting and assaults during the Ferguson crisis in Ferguson, MO.

Chris is currently the Senior Partner of Cebollero & Associates, a leadership/medical consulting firm. He is also a certified member of the John Maxwell Team.

RULE ONE

Never Allow Your Emotions to Dictate Your Actions

"The reputation of a thousand years may be determined by the conduct of one hour."

—A Japanese Proverb

There are ten rules of leadership described in this book. These "rules" of leadership come directly from my experiences as a leader. In the beginning, when I took on my first leadership role, I made many mistakes. It seemed like I was always doing things the hard way. It was frustrating, but I quickly realized that my mistakes came from a lack of experience.

Rule number one is: **Never allow your emotions to dictate your actions.** The Japanese proverb quoted in the chapter opening captures the truth in this fundamental rule of good leadership, it states: "The reputation of a thousand years may be determined by the conduct of one hour." Think about it, it takes forever to build up your leadership integrity, your leadership credibility. If you allow your emotions to dictate your actions, everything you've just built for all that time is now circling the drain until you can fix it.

I learned rule number one after I had a very emotional outburst with the members of my organization. I was frustrated and angry at the time. I was taking myself too seriously. The truth is, I wasn't a leader for the right reasons. The only reason I became a leader was because my organization asked me to be a leader. At the time, I wasn't doing anything that showed any good leadership characteristics.

I allowed the frustrations I was feeling to dictate my actions. I yelled and I pointed fingers. I talked bad about people. This type of behavior really affected me as a leader - instead of trying to nurture and guide I tore people down and played blame games. Instead of trying to help people be the best that they could be, I thought that they were there for *me*. In actuality, you realize that as a leader your job is to serve your employees and teams, to work for them, not for them to serve you and your career ambitions.

I allowed my emotions to dictate my actions and I paid the price of that for a lot of years. No matter how many times you say you're sorry to them, and how many times you try to rebuild your reputation back up, that cloud of your own history and actions never stops following you around.

Why We React with Emotions

It is important to stop for a moment and think about why we react with our emotions in the first place. When you think about a successful leader, what exactly are their characteristics? What are their specific attributes? This is someone that you have to completely trust, a person in authority that should also be easy to talk to and can be counted on to help when problems happen.

One of the most important attributes of a great leader is that they're able to make informed decisions and they're very decisive about that. One thing great leaders have in common is the fact that it takes a high degree of emotional intelligence to make decisive, informed decisions, keeping both the needs of the people and the business in mind. Most of us wouldn't think of leading using emotional intelligence as the cornerstone of good leadership.

We have to realize that how we react, our emotions, dictates how the people we work with at the office are going to feel about their workplace, the business itself and their job. If we're happy, they're happy. If we're pensive or on pins and needles, they're going to be on pins and needles. When you have a high degree of emotional intelligence, you're able to understand and manage your own emotions even when you are challenged or under stress. More importantly, you're able to understand and manage the emotions of the people that are around you as well.

Having a high level of emotional intelligence will give you a good understanding of your employee's feelings and what their motivations are, which is how we can figure out how to help them. As a leader, our job is to ensure that we're giving our employees the support that they need so they can give the customers the very best service.

When you're able to connect to people with emotional intelligence, it gives you a different level of respect for your employees. This level of understanding allows you to let them know that they're important to you and the organization. Employees need to feel that they're a valued and important member your team, contributing to the company's overall success.

It's in Your Brain Chemistry

Most people will be surprised to learn that you really have no choice but to react with emotions. Emotional reactions are actually based on how our body is made up. Our brains are wired to give us emotions. In our past as a species, sensing emotions gave us a survival advantage. Everything that we see, everything that we touch, everything that we hear, everything that we smell and taste—all our senses—is sent to our brain with electrical signals. These signals are then passed through the neurological system where they enter the brain at the base of the spinal cord.

What happens is, the signal needs to get to the frontal lobe, the front of the brain which is right behind the forehead where rational thinking and logic-based thinking take place. However, prior to it reaching the frontal lobe, that electrical signal passes through the limbic system. The limbic system is responsible for emotions and it is where our "fight or flight" response resides. It is because of this process in our body that we have no choice but to *feel* our emotional responses before we can process new information using logic or rational thought.

Take a Deep Breath

In order to use logical or rational thought, we must first learn to control our initial emotional response. One piece of advice that is commonly offered to achieve this is: if you feel yourself getting upset or nervous, take ten deep breaths or count to ten. This is to help you not act on the emotion before the emotion can get to the frontal lobe and trigger our rational and logical thought processes. It happens in the blink of an eye, but the fact is that a conscious pause gives you the opportunity not to react with emotion and allows your rational thinking to overcome the emotional response.

The limbic system and the frontal lobe influence each other, they work very closely and are in communication with each other, but regardless, the frontal lobe can't stop the emotions from being experienced. You're getting upset because your body is wired to get upset, it is wired to have those emotions happen, but you just need to realize that once it gets up into your logic area, the rational thought area, you should be able to think without your emotions taking over rational thought processes.

The Importance of Emotional Intelligence

Emotional intelligence is essential for leadership success. Leaders who shout or point fingers are reacting poorly to their own internal feelings and stress. Their followers aren't going to want to be part of that, it's going to decrease their motivation and that's going to reduce their employee engagement and job satisfaction. It also literally decreases their productivity. People want to follow leaders who are calm and one who they truly believe can lead them effectively during times of stress.

The Real Trap of Emotional Outbursts

No matter how I tried to get out from under that black cloud, my emotional outbursts to my workforce and to my team never really went away. Despite all the good that I did, it still hung over my head that I was someone who was short tempered. I was thought of as a bully, someone who didn't really care about the people in my workforce, but only myself.

It took literally years from that initial awakening incident when I first realized that I needed to change to overcome that lingering negative reputation. Three or four years later and regardless of my accomplishments, or my team's accomplishments, or how often we were recognized for the excellent work that we were doing, my negative reputation was always a black cloud hanging over my head.

Emotional intelligence and leading with emotional intelligence is a phrase describing a series of traits that a great leader must internalize and use as a base for all their actions, in good times or under stress. To gain a sense of emotional intelligence in your leadership style, it helps to first define how you react to things and why you react with emotional outbursts. You then ask yourself, how can I control these reactions? It teaches you how to understand the emotions that are going on around you.

Let's take the example of a common leadership moment during a routine business day. An employee or team member comes up to you and they're angry about the day, or they're frustrated. Maybe they are upset so they're going to raise their voice or they're going to point their finger. The first thing we want to do is we want to get defensive and do the same things back, but that isn't being a good leader and it doesn't solve their problem.

First, we need to remember how we tend to react in these types of situations. Then, we need to understand how others react in these types of stressful situations as well. We need to be able to use the five components of emotional intelligence to build up our leadership integrity and credibility, because when the going gets tough, nobody wants to follow somebody who is going to lose control and get angry and argue. They want to follow somebody that they trust to help them resolve their issue.

Once you're able to understand and put yourself in a position of **leading with emotional intelligence**, it becomes a part of your personal leadership toolbox.

Emotional Intelligence

As a leader, the more we can incorporate the components of emotional intelligence into our leadership style, the higher our emotional intelligence becomes. There are five main components to emotional intelligence: Self-Awareness, Self-Regulation, Motivation, Empathy and Social Skills. I will discuss each one individually.

Definition/Components of Emotional Intelligence:

1. Self-Awareness

2. Self-Regulation

3. Motivation

4. Empathy

5. Social skills

When we think about leading with emotional intelligence, first, we should have self-awareness. This is very important because this awareness helps you understand how your emotions effect the way you lead and what decisions you make in stressful moments. Often, we fail to notice how our emotions affect us, or the other people around us. We have to be aware of our emotions at all times.

There are times when you're driving to work and you're late getting out of the house, and you spill coffee on your shirt, you're in traffic and by the time you get to work you're a little bit flustered, you're a little bit frazzled and that shows on your face. Being self-aware is an important component in understanding your strengths and weaknesses as a leader. What is it that gives you that frown on your face? What is it that makes you smile? What is it that gives you anxiety? If you are able to identify and understand those things, it really gives you the opportunity to lead with humility rather than lead with your emotions.

Self-Awareness

One way that you can improve your self-awareness is by keeping a journal. This is what I did. Every time that I felt an emotion that was outside of my "normal," I wrote it down. I wrote in my journal about the specifics of the situation, describing what I thought made me feel an emotional reaction to it.

Then, in a moment of reflection, I'd go back to my journal and say, "Okay, now how did that make me feel? Why did this happen?" You should reflect on your day, you should reflect on your week, but you should also look through that journal to say, "How is it going to now help me grow as a leader?" You are now in a position to determine why you're reacting in certain ways if you're seeing it in front of you. You might think, "Oh, it's the same situation!" Or, discover, "Wow, every time this person comes in, I find myself getting a little bit edgy...maybe I need to do a little healing with that person." This will help you to understand yourself and gain a higher degree of self-awareness which is really important when you are striving to become a great leader.

Sometimes as leaders, we just need to take a time out. When we feel angry and our negative emotions are taking over our rational thinking, we need to learn to put ourselves in a little timeout. At that point, it's smart to take a walk to the water cooler, get a drink, make determinations about how we're feeling and decide how to react.

We've all sent that email off that we shouldn't send off and after we hit send, we're like, "What did I just do?" Being able to take that time out helps and ensures you're the one that controls how you react, not your emotions. Your limbic system is going to give you the emotion, but you determine if you want to react. With that brief break to reflect, you're able to choose and control your response.

Self-Regulation

Another part of emotional intelligence is self-regulation. Self-regulation is really the bridge between knowing that you're getting upset and staying in control and not letting it out. This is all about staying in control.

Do you react verbally when attacked? Do you get defensive when people come in and they point their finger at you? Knowing how you're going to react, do you make rushed or emotional decisions based on what's going on around you? A lot of people are knee-jerk leaders, and they make knee-jerk decisions when problems come up. They don't take the time to develop a solution.

Remember, in the beginning of this chapter, we talked about that Japanese proverb. It is vital we build our leadership credibility and not tear it down with one moment of allowing our emotions to dictate our actions. This is where your personal accountability comes in. There are things that irritate us, upset us, and make us frown, and give us those emotions every day, but being able to improve and be accountable to those emotions is what makes a valuable leader.

You can improve your ability to regulate yourself by knowing what your values are, knowing what you won't compromise. Write your own little personal code of ethics, write them down and post them somewhere, let everybody see them. You're not going to compromise your integrity, you're not going to compromise your trustworthiness. Those are important things to do to help you regulate yourself and you need to reflect on them regularly.

Remember, this is who you are. One of the things that we don't do well enough is we don't give ourselves good professional development and we don't stay true to ourselves as leaders. That's where we get into trouble. This will help you make the right choices. Once you compromise your morals, you're in trouble.

Motivation

Motivation is one of the toughest things that leaders have to do. It's not really motivation of the workforce, as much as it is self-motivation. Leading ourselves can be a real challenge sometimes. We think that it's easy—that we can hold other people to our expectations and hold other people accountable—but we don't really hold ourselves in that same way.

Being able to be self-motivated is a vital component to being a successful leader. It is this understanding that helps improve your emotional intelligence. Successful leaders are constantly working towards growth. Being growth-oriented means that you are always looking to learn, improve and move forward toward solutions. As leaders we need to be growth-oriented. We need to know that growing in our position is a journey that never ends and we never should want it to end.

Have high standards for yourself and know that you need to have high results for the quality and quantity of your work. Again, if you're going to be holding someone accountable to expectations, you need to exceed those expectations and be that role model for the people. There's a way to improve your motivation, that's to know who you are as a leader and why you are a leader. Are you a leader just because you're making more money? Or, are you a leader because you can rally the team, increase employee engagement and satisfaction, which will then increase productivity, which will then make your customers happier?

What's the purpose of you being a leader? You need to examine that. Regardless of the position you're in, you're a leader. You can be a janitor, you can be the CEO of the organization, you still need to lead people, but it starts by keeping yourself motivated. If you don't know what motivates you, there are a ton of leadership motivation assessments that are out there that can give you the opportunity to learn that.

Always be Optimistic

As good leaders, we also need to be able to be optimistic. When we only see the bad in things, our people are going to see the bad in them too. In rule number three we're going to talk about "there are no problems just solutions" which is an important part of being optimistic in the face of challenges and problems. We need to be able to take those challenges, those problems that we find and those bumps in the road of our day, and we need to accept them and be positive about them. We need to be able to ensure that our mentality stays positive. We all know those people, those "Negative Nelly's" that are in our organization that really bring people down. We're going to face challenges every day and we don't need people to have a negative effect on what we're doing. Learn from the things that are happening and help them be successful by maintaining a good positive and optimistic outlook.

Empathy

Empathy is one of those critical skills that we need to lead an organization. This is what enables us to put ourselves into the shoes of our employees and understand how they may see a situation. Leaders often talk about having an open door policy, and being there for employees. One of the rules that we're going to talk about later on is the importance of making time for employees.

We need to be able to put ourselves in the other's situation. In my career as a paramedic, I knew what it was like to live paycheck to paycheck. I knew what it was like to have problems with my schedule. I got a divorce. My kids were leaving town. I knew what it was like to sit in a truck with a partner for 12 hours a day and just wanting to stab him in the eye with a pencil just to get him to stop talking. When your workforce comes in and talks to you, what problems are they saying that are any different than what you've experienced when you were on that side of the desk? They're not any different. When they come in and talk about, "My wife is giving me challenges about my schedule," or "I'm going through a divorce," haven't we had similar experiences when we were employees? When we experienced those types of things, we wanted someone to listen to us. Sometimes we got it, and sometimes we didn't.

You're their role model, you're their leader. They want someone to listen and help with their problems. If you can, try to help. Part of being helpful in these situations is to understand where they want to go with their career and help them develop the skills they need to get there. Challenge the folks that are acting unprofessionally and say, "This attitude is not going to fly here. You need to be able to be the best that you can be so we can give the best to our customers."

Empathy is one of the best ways to earn respect in your organization as a leader. It also helps you develop the foundations of loyalty within your organization. Empathy is one of the most important components to good leadership.

When employees come to talk to you, be an empathetic listener. Show you care about them as a person and want to help. When someone is telling you their problem, you may know it's not an emergency, but the people who are coming to talk to you feel it's an emergency to them. You can blow it aside and say that this really is just a flash in a pan issue that will pass, but it's important to them. Put yourself in their position, and look at it from their perspective.

Another thing to do when someone is coming in and talking to you is not only monitor their body language, but yours as well. Remember, pay special attention to how you are reacting.

Ask yourself: How am I reacting as they tell me the story? How are they reacting as I'm giving them feedback? Are their arms crossed? Are they fidgeting? Watch their facial expressions. Ensure that the message is positive on both sides. Sometimes employees just need to vent.

I'll tell them to let me know that they have to vent and I'll say, "Okay, I'm going to give you seven minutes, you could just say whatever it is you want. Ready? Go." In my career of doing this, no one's ever gotten to seven minutes. Sometimes, they just need the opportunity to vent. Learn to read other's body language. That's going to be very telling and this is a real asset is when it comes to becoming a great leader.

Social Skills

Finally, social skills are a big part of emotional intelligence. Leaders that develop this component of emotional intelligence become, not only great leaders, but they also become great communicators.

Great communicators listen to good and bad news with an eye to solving problems and overcoming challenges, not placing blame. They're able to determine what the problems or challenges are and set a course to address the issues. They communicate well with their team, motivating them, creating excitement and inspiring the people around them. When we think about leadership, having the social skills necessary to influence people and being a great communicator are key aspects of a great leader.

Developing your social skills teaches you, not only how to respond, but it also helps you resolve issues and respond tactfully. Sometimes we don't do that, or in the heat of the battle, we blurt something out that comes out very harsh sounding. We didn't mean to sound harsh, but because we're involved in so many things that's the response they got from us. If you have good social skills, you can resolve the conflict tactfully, you won't leave things as they are, you'll go ahead and fix them in order to maintain a good working relationship.

We have the tendency as leaders to let problems linger and say, "Oh, they'll fix themselves." We'll, you've got your dice in your hand you're getting ready to roll and you better hope it comes up as seven because a lot of times it won't. Social skills are what helps you follow through and find solutions instead of waiting, hoping problems will simply go away or fix themselves. When you are a great leader, you don't just sit back while everyone else does the work. Instead, you know what needs to be done on the team and you're able to delegate appropriate resources to them in order to get the job done.

One of the things that developing your social skills will do for you is, it's going to set the example for others to follow. You are going to be calm, cool and collected. You're going to be able to take on challenges as they come up, respond to them, and deliver the best leadership that you can.

RULE TWO

Don't Waste Time And Energy On Things You Can't Control

"How much time have you wasted worrying about things that never came true?"

—*Chris Cebollero*

When I first became a leader, I wasted a lot of time and energy on things I can't control. I'd be imagining the worst case scenario in every situation and I'd stress myself out with endless worry. It was a long time before I learned this lesson and added to my personal leadership toolbox.

In my life, I wanted to be able to control every aspect of my day, my work and what my team was doing at all times. The reality is, there are things that we just can't control. Personally, I don't think that we can really control anything.

Great leadership is about being able to listen and respond in a positive way. It's about moving forward and solving problems as they come up. When I was just starting out as an inexperienced leader, I would spend too much time worrying and wondering what might happen tomorrow. Back then I caused myself a lot of my own stress.

Tomorrow is going to come regardless of what we spend our time thinking about and if we spend time and energy on things we can't control, we are truly wasting our time. Stop for a moment and think about how much time you spend worrying. If we took that same amount of time that we waste worrying about things and instead, focused our thoughts on something more positive, think how much more successful you would be.

Seven Ways to Know you are a Control Freak

- Your team struggles to share new ideas
- You think you're wonderful
- You always know you're right
- You control organizational information
- You are part of every decision
- You can't let go of the reins
- You ARE the final authority—on every decision

Are you one of those employees or leaders that always worry about what's going on at work? Do you tell yourself stories about what hasn't even occurred yet but might occur? Do you make up worst case scenario fantasies in your mind? These are all traits of people with a need to control everything around them.

I've got a friend of mine who can develop a story about the unknown like nobody's business. Chatting with her recently, it was clear to me that she was suffering from excessive worry and the need to be constantly in control. It reminded me of how I used to be when I first become a leader. Back then, I couldn't let anything be out of my control.

It happened that she had been trying to reach her daughter all morning who was away at college. The first "story" she shared was, she must be in class and would give a call back soon. After there had still been no call back within a few hours, she had called again with no answer. Now her story changes, she thinks maybe her daughter is out with her friends. Soon that story morphed into, maybe her car's broken down or maybe she's on the side the road somewhere. Then she's asking herself, What if the wrong person stopped to help her? Finally, her story-telling imagination says her daughter might be laying in a ditch somewhere, dead.

Of course, we came to find out that she was taking a nap at the time and the ringer on her phone was off. But, when we are people with a strong need to control everything around us, we spend a lot of time developing these "stories" in our mind. Our imagination allows those stories to control the situation for us. Instead, we need to start thinking about how we can allow things to happen and react and respond to them as they as they occur.

The Psychology of Control Freaks

We need to understand that as human beings we are very complicated individuals. We have a deep need to have a sense of control over our lives and what happens to us. When we feel like things are out of control, this causes feelings of stress and tension. Uneasiness and uncertainties keep us up at night worrying about the future and replaying the past mistakes and regrets we have. Everyone has a need to control their own reality, however, some people have such a strong need to maintain control that it takes over much of their time and hinders their success in life. Wanting to be in control to that extent usually comes some deep-rooted history, fears or negative experiences that happened in life.

Why are Some People so Controlling?

- They lost control somewhere in their lives
- To feel superior
- To resist control attempts
- Fear of abandonment
- To prove something

Some people want to be controlling because subconsciously they want to feel bigger and better. It is possible that they lost control of their life at some point in the past. Maybe there is some emotion that occurred in the past that they don't want to feel again and subconsciously, if they're in control, that feeling won't occur.

There are warning signs of becoming too controlling that we need to think about as leaders. If we're trying to control the things around us too much, folks become apprehensive, they won't bring us their ideas. They won't come in and share their visions with us. That really hurts our ability to lead. If we have an ego, if we think we're the cat's meow, the top of the food chain, that feeling of superiority is going to show and people are going to know that you're not really out to help them, but only advance yourself.

Controlling the Information

What if it's that you're not being transparent as a leader? What if what you're controlling is information, do you enjoy keeping people in the dark? The thing about control is, if we don't empower others to succeed, we're really the ones that are going to fail. Sharing information is vital for our team to trust us and follow us as their leader. If you think you might have a problem with control, it is important to learn specific ways to give up control.

Delegation of Authority

Of the ten most common leadership mistakes is failing to delegate authority to people in our organization. Coming from a control freak who used to try to control everything, this is going to be a hard adjustment, but remember this is not about you, you became a leader in the organization and you have to *lead* the organization, not *control* it. Take your ego out of the equation. Grow your team, allow them to make mistakes and learn from them. Be sure to allow your workforce to take credit for their accomplishments, don't steal that credit for yourself. Highlight their skills and their expertise to others. And, delegate tasks to others and do not interfere while they do them.

Delegation of authority is something that is important to your leadership success. Not only are you taking things off your plate, but you're teaching the leaders of tomorrow. Instead of looking at them as being a workforce, look at them as future leaders of the organization. As you develop good delegation skills, you are now growing your team which increases their leadership effectiveness and team productivity.

Delegation of authority is when you give your empowerment, your authority to someone to complete a goal, a task, a process, or a project. One of the mistakes, control oriented leaders make is trying to stand over their shoulder and micromanage them as they complete a task or project. One mistake I made as a leader taught me this lesson the hard way and I've added it to this rule for great leadership.

When you Delegate, Stand Back and let Them do the job

I had given one of my team members a project to do and they said, "What your vision for this?" I said, "My vision is that we want to be able to be effective and cost-efficient," but I gave no other details. Every so often I would check on the process and every so often I would ask, "How things are going?" But, I didn't follow through with any details. Then, at the end when the project was submitted to me, I made this comment which was really taken the wrong way—they asked me, "What do you think? How does it look?" I said, "This is not the way I would have done it..." It wasn't about me at that point, it was about a team member who was taking on something new and was asking for feedback from me. Actually, her development of the project was a lot better than what I would have done, but that isn't how it came out! She understood it as, "She didn't do it as well as I would have done."

When we give our empowerment to other people, however they get the job completed, we have to be able to accept that and only offer constructive feedback on the result. Then, we can guide them and help their skills along without making them feel defensive. If there's a component missing in the project that they're not seeing, stand back and allow them make mistakes. Allow them to experience that and to grow from their experience without reaching for that sense of control you'd get from taking over for them.

Giving up Control

- Letting go of your ego
- Delegate authority
- Recognize you cannot control everything

Giving up Control

People always say to me, "What if I fail?" **Failure isn't falling down; failure is forgetting to get up.** Let them fail, let them learn. When we are mentoring others, our failed experiences that we share with our mentee help them avoid the mistakes that we made along the way. Our positive experiences that we've learned throughout our career, give them clues about what might work for them. We all really do learn best from our experiences.

Controlling Fears

- Recognition
- Identify your fears
- Be inquisitive
- Stay positive

Don't Allow Yourself to be Afraid

Don't allow yourself to be afraid. Beware of the "What if…" trap. In the workforce, our weekly scare, the story we tell ourselves goes something like this: What if it's not good enough? What if they're going to replace me? What if I made a mistake? What if…? What if…What if…? I always remember this quote from the movie "Remo Williams: The Adventure Begins" (1985), the character Chiun says to Remo when he is teaching him martial arts, "Fear is just a feeling. You feel hot. You feel hungry. You feel angry. You feel afraid. Fear can never kill you."

Being afraid is not going to hurt you. Learning the skill of dealing with your fears is something that anyone can accomplish. One of the biggest challenges is that most people hold on to their emotions. They make them part of their inner foundation, their beliefs about themselves, which ultimately gives fear control.

The Bottom Line is:

Fear is the enemy to our success and we need to be able to ensure that we become partners with our fear so that we can overcome its power.

You're always going to have anxieties and apprehensions, but you've got to learn to be partners with those fears. Learn to keep them exactly where they need to stay—as passing thoughts and not as agents of control.

When you're directed by your fears, you'll never take the risks that catapult your career to the next level. Les Brown says: "Life has no limitations, except the ones that you make." We set limitations on ourselves.

We've got to learn to control our fears. We need to recognize our fears and make sure that we know exactly what they are—and, we must find out why we feel the things that we're feeling so we can overcome the fear that holds us back from success.

The feeling we have is—"I'm going to lose control!" But, **facing your fears is like playing a game**. You've got to think many moves ahead and eventually that strategy is going to help you win. The thing is, you can't do it if you're worried about what's behind every corner, there are things that are going to pop up that are going to be challenging, but if you go through the steps of problem solving you can figure them out.

Respect Your gut Feelings

Any time we have a gut feeling, we've got to respect our feeling because for some reason the subconscious is saying, "You know what, be cautious." But when I talk about fear, I'm talking about the **fear of the unknown**, **anxiety**, the **"what if"** trap. What if... the Starship Enterprise comes and beams me aboard? Well, when that happens we'll deal with it, but until then, let's not waste time and energy on things we can't control.

Recognize you Cannot Control Everything

Going back to my story about my friend— remember, it starts off where she can't reach her daughter at college and before she finally gets in touch and learns that her daughter is okay, she's imagined that her daughter is dead in a ditch by somebody who pulled over to help her after her car broke down. It those types of fears that waste our time and energy endlessly.

In the beginning of this chapter I asked, "How much time have you wasted on things that never came true?" When we are stuck thinking and worrying, when we think about our fears and worry over those thoughts and stories we are only hurting ourselves.

Even though we've developed a great imagination, built up stories in our mind, those stories we told ourselves never, ever came true. They didn't help us *do* anything, *build* anything or *move forward in life* in any way. If you are a controlling leader, a worrier, or a story teller, develop a plan for yourself to change.

RULE THREE

There are no problems, JUST solutions

"Don't find fault, find the remedy."

—*Henry Ford*

Steps of Problem Solving

- Define the problem
- Determine the root cause
- Create many possible solutions
- Select a solution
- Implement the solution
- Evaluate the outcome

As a leader, I used to be guilty of pointing fingers. I'd be asking: Who did that? Why did that happen? How come this happened? Who's responsible for this kind of thing? I eventually realized that for everything that happened throughout my leadership day, I only saw the problems.

I'd be problem-focused all day long. Quick, the ambulances have to get in for an inspection. Wait, we'd better take care of preventive maintenance or else they might break down, so we've got the two ambulances down. Great, we're already crunched on the staff scheduling and now we've got EMTs and paramedics who have called out sick. I'd be thinking, how are we going to get the trucks on the street? Everything was a problem. Everything that occurred, I took on as being trouble. I instantly saw it as being the worst thing that could happen. It wasn't an effective way to lead or healthy for me personally.

Problems vs. Challenges

A realization came to me as I was a learning how to be an effective manager/leader, as these problems were occurring I didn't even call them problems anymore. I called them challenges. We can overcome a challenge. A problem is just a negative word that doesn't move us forward.

Changing the Paradigm

My leadership team doesn't come to me and say, "I have a problem," they come and say, "We've got a challenge." They say, "We need solutions." Throughout my leadership career the rule was confirmed: there are no problems, just solutions.

Leaders and Future Leaders

As I addressed these problems as challenges, I became a more effective leader. I was almost waiting for challenges to happen so I could grow my leadership knowledge and expand my base of core knowledge. There are problems that happen within our workforce and in our organization every day. We need to be able to go through the steps of problem solving, and turn the things that we see as challenges into solutions. Ultimately, this grows our organization which then grows our own leadership ability.

Get Many Different People Involved in Problem Solving

When you're developing a plan for problem solving, you need to make sure that you get as many people involved as possible. This approach is a key to developing a problem solving culture in your organization. Allow the group to help you manage the process. As these challenges occur, not only are you helping your organization but you're showing the future leaders who are coming up behind you that when these things occur this is the problem solving process, and how you work together as a team to solve the problem.

An example would be, during the crisis in Ferguson, Missouri, I was in charge of the medical control to ensure that everybody received the highest quality of patient care. As these problems were happening, I put a junior leader, one of my Operations Supervisors in charge of the medical control. Now, a lot of people will point a finger and they'll say, "Wait a minute! You were the most experienced person on the scene! Why are you giving up that medical control to somebody who doesn't have that experience?" But, I thought, "What a great opportunity for them to have problems occur, deal with it, yet have somebody who is more experienced just a few feet away that they can bounce their ideas off!"

So the lesson is, get a group involved, solve the problems as efficiently as you can and make sure that you come up with the best solution. Problem solving steps can be repeated at any time. The process is a continuous process. Keep in mind, however, that just because the problem seems solved, doesn't mean you don't need to follow up to ensure that it doesn't happen again.

Define the Problem

The first component to solving the problem is: Define what the problem is, and how does it affect the processes? Ask the questions: How did this happen? Whose area of responsibility is this? How long has this problem been an issue?

For example, has the pipe been leaking for the past six months or did it just start leaking? A word of caution, get into the habit of not pointing fingers at a department or individuals. Develop the mentality of not assigning blame, but instead just address the problem. Your workforce will appreciate that effort. Find out why it occurred and over what period of time. It is not enough to say, "I don't know, I just found out today." You need to know, is this the first time it happened or has this been ongoing?

Normalization of Deviance

There is a concept called the "normalization of deviance" and the normalization of deviance happens when we have a process and within that process sometimes we're not doing all of the steps of that process. Maybe there are ten steps and we're really only doing nine steps. Soon, nine becomes the new normal and then, over a period of time, we're only doing eight steps. Now, eight becomes the new normal. We need to be able to identify why this problem occurred and then determine the root cause of why it occurred.

Determine the Root Cause of the Problem

When there is a problem, determine the root cause. Exactly what were the steps that occurred (or were missed) that caused this problem to come about? There are specific problem solving processes that you can use to determine the root cause of a problem.

You might use a Fishbone Diagram, Pareto Chart, DMAIC (Define-Measure-Analyze-Improve-Control), or create a Five Why's Diagram. These are proven methods. Find the one that works for you. I would encourage you to learn them all and as these challenges come up, you'll be able to use different problem solving techniques.

Once you get to that point of understanding the problem, the timing and why it occurred at this specific time, you need to create several possible solutions. These potential solutions have to be based on facts and on what you think the best result will be. This should not be a solution you come up with as an immediate reaction to a problem or challenge. You need to take your time to develop the solution.

Generate as many potential solutions as you can, relate each solution to what the specific problem was and the cause of the problem. Also, don't forget to think about similar things that have happened in the past. For example, you might say something like, "When we had the problem with the generator the last time, we found out that it was sitting in two feet of water so we just lifted it up. Maybe that's a possible solution that we could use in this case as well..."

Choose the Best Solution

At this stage you need to be able to choose what you think is the best solution to try, but remember, just because you choose this solution be ready to change tactics if this solution fails to meet the problems needs.

One of the things that you have to realize is that what you come up with may fail and that's okay. It's not about wasting time, you went ahead and tried to come up with the best solution that you could and the challenge was, it just didn't work. Let's go back to the drawing board and do it again. In our analytical mind, I don't think we take that idea very well. We don't like feeling like we've failed.

Experience = You Might not Come up With the Right Solution the First Time

You've got to remember that in order to gain experience, the fact is, you may not come up with the correct solution the first time, and that's okay. That's how we learn. This is how we gain experience, and develop foresight. We remember what we tried in the past that worked and what didn't work. This experience helps us to make different decisions later.

Once you figure out what you're going to do, you need to implement a solution and to ask yourself: What must be done? Who's going to do it? How is it going to be started? How do we know when we've gotten to the point that we've corrected this problem? Who is it that's going to carry out these actions? Who's responsible for making sure that all this was implemented?

Get Different People Involved in Problem Solving and Creating Solutions

Get different people involved in this process. I have to ask myself, as the leader: Is this my responsibility to be the one to up fix this for somebody? It could be. But, if I'm the one who directs a team to solve the problem, then I'm developing somebody's critical thinking skills. I'm developing their problem solving skills.

When you develop the critical thinking and problem solving skills of the people in your workforce, they may not even need to bring their challenges to your office anymore. But instead, they might just brief you on what they found, how they addressed it, and the outcome. This shows initiative and growth.

Constant Evaluation of our Solutions to Problems

After you've implemented a solution, you need to evaluate the outcome. One of the failures that we have as leaders, and as organizations is that we will put something into place and just assume that it went according to plan and that everything is working out well. Instead, we've got to be able to ensure that we put an evaluation and monitoring process into this new solution.

For example, if we we've changed the whole workflow for a process and we need to know what we did was right we have to monitor the results. We may have identified the problem, found out why it occurred, came up with some great solutions and implemented those solutions, but in the end, we could realize that we really didn't come up with a solution at all.

This is where that evaluation comes in and we should ensure that we're looking at it on a regular basis. This is something we should come back two months later, six months later and even one year later to say, "Hey, remember we put that process in place to ensure that the trucks got their inspections on time or their preventive maintenance on time? Let's go and look at that process to see how it works." There's an old saying that says, "If it's not broke, don't fix it," I don't believe in that. I believe in challenging your processes. When you challenge your process, you know that the solutions you put into place are going to work.

Decisive Leaders

There are five techniques to become a decisive leader.

Five Techniques to Become a Decisive Leader

    1) Be fully accountable

    2) Make the vision a reality

    3) Ask the right questions

    4) Make decisions

    5) Be Confident in your decisions

Be Fully Accountable

The first one is to be fully accountable. As a decisive leader, you have to be accountable to your workforce and to your organization. But, you also have to be accountable to developing the leaders who are coming up behind you.

You do this by giving your employees opportunities to grow their problem solving skills and their critical thinking skills. You need to give them the autonomy to make decisions. By giving them the opportunity to solve challenges, you're giving them the ability to grow, to make mistakes and to be successful.

Remember you need to know that the buck stops with you when it comes to accountability. You are ultimately responsible for the failures of the team. When they are successful as a team, ensure the team gets all the credit, when there are failures and mistakes take all the blame and protect your workforce.

Now with that said, you still have to make certain that you are holding your team accountable. Give them the opportunities to learn, grow and gain the needed experience. When you are holding the workforce accountable, this will begin the process of increasing the wins in the organization.

Others are going to depend on you, they are going to follow you. They're going to trust you and they're going to show you their accountability because now you've just set that expectation. Even though you're sitting at the top of the organization you have to be accountable as well.

Don't be an organization that doesn't allow the workforce to take credit for success. Middle managers, allow your leadership team to take the lead on making each project a success.

I could sit with my hands behind my head and my feet on the desk and make all the decisions. But, what I want to be able to do is empower the people who are around me to be able to make decisions. It all starts with being fully accountable.

Make the Vision a Reality

Decisive leaders also need to be able to see the vision, we have to know how to get there and be able to help people understand what their role is in that vision and then work toward it together. A lot of leaders fail at helping the vision come through. As leaders, we need to be value based. We need to be driven toward a clear purpose. We need understand what our role is. Our role is creating an environment to support the growth of the people on our teams and in the organization.

The Secret Sauce

The secret sauce is to being a successful leader is to grow the workforce, value them, give them the tools they need to be successful and then allow them to do the work. We hired these people into our organizations to help the organization be successful and yet we keep them at arm's reach. We keep them at a distance when we want them to try to help grow our organization. It's our role to give them the tools, to give them the opportunities to be successful and then get out of their way and let them do it. Unfortunately, we fail at that sometimes. We need to be able to operate with purpose. We need to have our values firmly in our mind and we need to be able to share that with our workforce.

Ask the Right Questions

Often, we don't ask the right questions. There are some leaders that I've talked to in my career that only ask questions when problems come to their office. Instead of giving direction to their teams and trying to help the team identify solutions, they're giving answers and directions.

They need to be asking more questions and allowing the people who brought the issue to come up with the solutions themselves. When you're a decisive leader, you gather facts, analyze situations, and determine advantages and disadvantages. You allow the people who are around you to help you come up with those answers based on the questions that you've asked them. When you use this strategy, they're going to be able to solve problems effectively by themselves one day.

Make Decisions

Finally, one of the things that marks a decisive leader is the ability to make decisions. A lot of times, it seems like leaders will hang on to making decisions for too long. We've got to be able to ensure that our decisions are timely.

We're going to make mistakes sometimes when we make decisions. We need to be able to say, "Well, it didn't work. Back to the drawing board." Most people think that it's bad to do that, but if you make a decision, and fail at it, it's best if you stand up and say, "Well, that didn't work very well and then find something else."

You're going to be more respected if you do that than if you wait days or weeks to come up with a decision. If you wait too long, sometimes you forget you've promised someone that you'd make a decision. Then, the news of the decision you promised to make never comes to the person who has been waiting for it.

Be Confident in Your Decisions

We have to be confident in what we've already done or decided. A lot of indecisiveness comes from a lack of confidence. We've got to be comfortable enough with who we are and with the information that we've used to make our decisions to feel confidence in our choices. Then, we can decide and move forward with confidence. We must believe that we were able to make the best decision we could at the time, with the information we had in front of us.

RULE FOUR

Develop a Vision

"The only thing worse than being blind is having sight but no vision."

– Helen Keller

Defining Your Vision

Creating a vision with a formal vision statement to drive the organization is one of the most important things you can do to direct the future success of the organization. This process clarifies the values and the direction of the department or organization and shows people where they fit into the overall mission that the company hopes to accomplish.

Why is Having a Vision Important?

The organizational vision is a key component to the success of any organization. We have to be able to give our members a visual picture of where we are going and how they need to get there. My friend and mentor John Maxwell teaches that we think in pictures. He will ask you to close your eyes and then he'll say, "Think of your front door…now I want you to think about your car." He continues, "When you thought about door, you actually saw the picture of your door. When you thought about your car, you didn't see the word CAR, you saw the picture of your car…" This lesson shows that as individuals we think in pictures. If organizations do not have a vision that is front and center to guide our workforce, they will not have a visual picture of where the organization is heading, or what they are working towards.

Since we're wired to think in pictures, in the absence of a vision of where we're going, the workforce and the leadership team would have no idea where the organization was going or what it ultimately was trying to achieve. Since we need visual information to process ideas, we've got to be able to disseminate the vision to the people who do the work so they can understand how it fits into their roles and duties. This is why having an active vision statement is a vital component of our organizational success.

Communicate Your Vision

When I became the Chief of EMS at Christian Hospital, I came into the department and realized that they had no vision statement. I gathered people from the workforce and I put them around a table and I asked, "What's our mission here? What do we do? Where are we going?" And the common response was, "We relocate the sick and injured." "Okay, what else do we do?" There was really no vision of where we were going to go as an organization, no bigger picture or purpose in their minds.

Getting Feedback on the Vision

We sat down as a team and we came up with three vision statements. I said, "I want to know who you are. I want to know where we're going and I want to know who we're going to become." Three vision statements came from that meeting. We sent those out to the workforce and we said, "Now, vote on the one you want."

The vision chosen was that we were going to give the highest quality of patient care. We were going to be leaders in our community. And, we were going to be role models for our career field.

Everything that we did as a department, I would always ask the question, "How does that help us reach the vision?" Someone would say, "We need to bring this new educational program here." I'd ask, "How does this help us reach the vision?" Another person would say, "We need this new piece of equipment here." Again, I'd ask, "How does this help us reach our vision?" Everything was steeped into the vision.

When the Ferguson Riots broke out in Missouri in 2014, our vision statement was front and center when we decided how to handle that volatile situation. We were thinking, how do we handle this civil disobedience and being right in the middle of rioting and looting and assaults yet providing an emergency service to both sides of the conflict with the highest degree of professionalism? Everything went back to our vision statement. **"We're going to deliver the highest quality of patient care. We're going to be leaders in our community. We're going to be role models for our career field."**

One of the most common things about most company vision statements is– they aren't used. I'll talk to leaders and ask them, "How many of your organizations have a vision statement?" All the leaders will raise their hand. I say, "How many people can recite it for me?" No one.

My question to you as a leader is: "If *you* can't recite the vision statement, how can your employees recite the vision statement and how can they know where they're going?"

When we talk about the development of the vision, this is a road map, a blueprint for the success of the organization and how you're going to get there.

Developing a Vision Statement

Now that you've read this chapter, maybe you don't know what your vision statement is. This is a great opportunity to start a campaign, get your workforce together, get your leadership team together, and say, "Here's our vision statement. Is it what we need to do now and into the future?" Rewrite it, and create a campaign and post it up in the department and put it on little cards and make sure everybody knows what the vision is.

This is an Opportunity:

You read books like this and you take leadership

classes to get better at being a leader. Here's a great secret – develop yourvision statement with your workforce. Develop your vision statement with your leadership team. Have them vote on it.

Develop a campaign around it and make it part of your marching orders as you go forward.

Vision

When it comes to developing your vision statement, you want to try to get as many people involved in the process as possible. As leaders, we often talk about getting buy-in from our workforce for new ideas. Getting them involved, getting them a seat at the table is something that is very important but you need to be able to know where your organization is heading and how they are going to get there.

You need to be able to determine what is it that you want to do, what is it that you want to give. Is it a service? Is it a product?

When you create a vision, this is the big dream, this is the leap into the ultimate achievement. The old quote of "A goal is a dream with a deadline" comes into play here. When you work towards making your vision a reality, those goals come with a deadline as well. Think about the big things that you can do and where the organization needs to go and what's important to accomplish those goals when you discuss your vision statement.

When meeting my workforce for the first time, my goal was to set the foundation for success right from the beginning of our relationship together. My comments to them were that if they followed me, and worked and developed together as a team, that we would eventually compete and win the National EMS Service of the Year Award. In 2014, we became the top EMS Agency in the United States, and our vision came true.

Developing a Personal Vision

Where do you want to get to and how are you going to get

there? How does your personal vision fit in the organizational vision? When we think about who we are as people, keep in mind that, if the vision statement of the organization goes against our personal values then we aren't going to be able to do the best job we can. As leaders, we have to be able to ensure that our vision statement is really part of the personal values of all the people that are going to live by it as well.

Look at how Your Vision Contributes to Your Community

Part of your vision statement should also take into account what's happening within your community. Take into account what's happening within your organization as well. If you're a department within an organization, you need to ask, "How does your vision to fit into the strategic goals of the organization?" If you're in an organization that serves a community, ask, "What's the vision for the community and how can we help make that a reality?" You want to think about who you are, where you're going, where you want to be and how to get there. You know the vision statement isn't about getting to the vision, the vision statement is the *journey* you take in getting to the vision.

Help Take Ownership in the Vision

For an organization to be successful, it is crucial that everyone take an active role and ownership of the vision. It's important for an organization to think about who they are, think about where the organization is heading, and once they reach that vision, who they will become. When everyone has a stake in the vision, they can work together to make it a reality.

When you're trying to reach your vision, be courageous and know that you want to do something that's going to stretch and grow both the workforce and the organization itself.

You want to do something that is going to challenge you. The people that are coming into today's workforce will be working for the next forty-five years. It is our role as leaders to give them the vision necessary to be inspired and motivated to become part of a winning team.

Make the Vision Dynamic and Fluid

What you're striving for is a creative vision that challenges you to get things done, to be the best that you can be. Your workforce will appreciate it. One of the things you may have to do initially is, you may have to modify that vision as time goes on and situations change.

Sometimes you come up with something that's too strict. When developing your vision statement ensure this is not set in stone and instead, make it a dynamic document of future success. In the health care industry, it seems like something is changing every single day. If you had a vision statement that was stagnant are you going to be able to change your strategic goals to meet the changing environment?

Change and transition may be part of your career field as well. When your vision statement allows for updates and tweaks to meet the changing transitions, this is what will keep your organization moving to meet the needs of the community it serves. Look at your vision statement regularly and determine if changes in your field require you to consider a different direction to meet the changing times.

RULE FIVE

Make Time For Employees

"Leadership is lifting a person's vision to high sights, the raising of a person's performance to a higher standard, the building of a personality beyond its normal limitations."

—Peter Drucker

Make Time for Employees

In my early years as a leader, people would come to my office looking for my guidance, wanting my mentorship, or who needed my support. My mistake was not making time for them, and sending them away. The only thing this helped me gain was resentment from my workforce.

Eventually I noticed, they stopped coming to me with their issues and challenges. My actions caused me to have the reputation of someone that did not care about his people. My day was otherwise more important to me, rather than to help them with their problems, or whatever issues they had.

There was no teaching on my part or assisting with growth. Needless to say, my leadership effectiveness suffered. My workforce did not care about me or the organization because I did not care about them. Eventually, I realized that I needed to change my approach by making more time for my employees.

When I shared what I had just learned with my mentor he said, "Why are you inviting people to your organization that you don't care about?" I was confused. I asked, "What do you mean by inviting people to your organization?" My mentor explained. "You've hired them. These people came to you and you looked at them and said, 'Come here and help my organization be successful.'"

I still didn't get it. Then, my mentor said to me, "You're just giving them a job, is that it? All you care about is giving them a job?" That was a real wake up call for me because I realized that for me to be successful, I needed to make time for my employees. My leadership role is to give them whatever they need to be successful. That's why I created leadership rule number five: "Make time for employees."

My Four Questions

- What can I do for you today?
- If you were the leader of this department, what is the one thing you would change and why?
- How can I help you reach your goals?
- What advice do you have for me to become a better leader for you?

When you make time for employees, this gives employees the opportunity to just chat about whatever is important to them. My role wasn't to manage the budget, my role wasn't to meet with lawmakers; my role was to take care of those employees that were doing the job. I asked people who came into my office one of the following questions: What can I do for you today? If you were the leader of this department, what is the one thing you would change and why? How can I help you reach your goals? What advice do you have for me to become a better leader for you?

Evaluations Every 90 days

We also gave evaluations every 90 days instead of annually.

These take a little bit more work for the leadership team, but it ensures that the leaders have to get in front of the employees, at least for an hour. To give a review every 90 days, the department leaders now had to ensure they were meeting with the workforce more regularly and assisting them in reaching their quarterly goals.

Second thing that 90 day reviews did was help employees reach their goals. Because we were meeting regularly, we knew where they wanted to go and we wanted to help them reach their goals. Every 90 days we were saying, "Where are you on your goals? How can we help you reach your goals?"

The third thing 90 days reviews led to was that employees weren't surprised at the end of the year with their evaluation. Instead of going over goals once a year in the typical annual review, we were talking about goals and challenges all year round. Since the formal communication of goals and progress was happening every 90 days between the employee and the leadership team, we always knew how much progress had been made and exactly how we were going to be able to help each employee reach their goals.

If we were talking about being late three times, or said, "You didn't deliver great patient care here," we were then able to work with them and say, "How are you now able to change this for the next 90 day term?"

Get to Know Your Employees

Getting to know your employees personally is also something that is very, very important. You don't need to go out and have a beer or go out to dinner, but you need to develop a friendly, cordial professional relationship with them.

You need to understand who they are and their personal motivations. I always ask this question to leadership groups: "How many of the leaders out there have employees that have families?" You see a lot of hands go up. Then I ask: What are their names? You see a blank look on their faces. Too many leaders don't make the time to get to know their employees as people.

Understanding who your employees are as people outside of work helps you understand how to connect with them and creates the kind of trust that a leader needs to be successful.

You're Their Role Model/Mentor

You've also got to remember, you are their role model. You're their mentor. You're the one that they want to come to and ask for your guidance, ask for your mentorship to say, "How do I deal with this situation?"

Facebook

One of the best tools ever made for leaders is Facebook. I don't go out and solicit my workers to be my Facebook "friends," but if they want me to be their friend, I certainly accept their friendship on Facebook. I can see what the employee did that weekend and who took their kid to their first hockey game or who went on a skiing vacation. Then when I see those employees around the organization, I am able to talk to them about their life, family, and activities outside of the office. I might say, "That looked like a really great ski trip!" Or, "Wow, was that your kid's first hockey game?" That level of caring about the person and not just their role in the organization goes a long way toward earning the respect of your employees.

Be Authentic

Don't forget to be authentic as you get to know your employees. Let them get to know a little bit about yourself and your personal life as well. It is important to be able to relate to each other on a person-to-person level in the workplace.

If you're the leader, you've invited these people into your organization. You need to become their role model, you have to guide them towards success and it's important that you demonstrate the characteristics and behaviors we want others to display at work. Remember, how we treat our workforce sets the tone and attitude within the organization. You've got to be able to demonstrate the characteristics and behavior that we want other people to display at work.

Be Transparent

You need to be transparent as well. Is there anything that's in the organization that we can or can't share with our workforce? Generally, the only thing we should not discuss is people's personal issues, challenges or mistakes within the department. We should, however, talk about budget, available resources, hiring plans, openly and as transparently as possible. This open form of communication will not allow rumors or the grapevine mentality to fester. They are hearing organizational information from you directly. This openness needs to be at every level of the organization, not just the leadership team.

Employees need us to act transparently as leaders. We need to share as much as we can of the information that we have access to—whenever it is appropriate to do so. When the employees know exactly where the organization is, this decreases speculation and fear. As a leader, I believe that the workforce does not work for me. Instead I work for them, to give them what they need to be successful, to learn and grow. I'm working for them, it is my responsibility to be as transparent and share the leadership information about what's going on.

Be Visible in Your Workforce as a Leader

Be sure to also be visible, be out in the workforce and in their work areas. As a paramedic and as a Chief of EMS, a lot of the workforce was scattered around throughout the city. It was important for me to travel to where they were working and see them in their environment. We had an open door policy, this was to make sure the leaders were visible and accessible to everyone.

Be Flexible

An open door policy means if my door is open, you're free to come in and interrupt me and say that you need something from me. When an employee came to my door and I was on the phone, regardless of who I was talking to, I'd hang up. I would turn off my computer monitor. I would set my phone aside. Sometimes people come into your office to talk and that's an opportunity for developing a genuine relationship between employees and leadership. This kind of openness and flexibility inspires trust and builds an *esprit de corps*. Building camaraderie creates the level of trust that you need to be able to grow people into future leaders. They need to know that you have their best interests in mind as you're taking care of leadership responsibilities within the organization.

Give Kudos

We need to engage with employees and offer positive feedback, not just in day-to-day conversations, but every time we see them. Give kudos. Think about how the results or the work that each employee does contributes to your organization.

One of the best practices we did in the organization occurred during our weekly leadership meetings. Every Tuesday at 7 am, before we began our agenda every leader on the team, had to bring an employee kudos to the group. This was always our first order of business. The supervisor would announce why their employee was being recognized that week. That supervisor would then have to write a hand-written thank you note to that employee, and when the rest of the leadership team saw that employee, we patted them on the back for their recognition. There were eight leaders in the organization recognizing the employee's efforts.

Say Thanks

We need to say thanks to our employees, lead by example, ask for input and give praise regularly. That is the crux of developing a positive work environment, making time for your employees and showing them that they're not just employees, but that they really are the backbone to the success of the organization.

Looking back, that when I was an inexperienced leader I felt like I had more important things to do than to listen to and help my employees. I had a sense of wanting to "fix" things for people, but also a sense of frustration. I'd be thinking, "This is the third time we've talked about this issue, how many times are we going to address it?" It wasn't that I was truly apathetic to the employee's needs as much as it was that I was feeling put out—as if they were bothering or interrupting me when I had (what I saw) as "more important" things to do.

Ask for Input

I can look back and remember talking with people where I needed their input and I needed their guidance and it became clear when people weren't really listening to me.

So, when I thought a Supervisor was not listening to me, as a test I would throw some random and obscure piece of information in just to see if I was correct. For example, when talking to a Supervisor about a budget issue, I would throw a random *"Oompa Loompa"* into my description just to see if they would catch it!

It makes you realize that not listening is really a bad trait for a leader to have. Here's the thing, I learned that I was precipitating the problem by not listening to my employees in the first place.

When we have an open-door policy, you're there for them anytime that they want to come in. You're saying, "My door is always open for you." That includes your ability to be an active listener and to give them the respect that they deserve for sharing their opinions and their feelings with you.

Encourage Personal Growth

Encourage personal growth and help your employees get to where they want to be within the organization, or in their career. If it's college they are interested in pursuing, let's make it easy for them to get to college. The easier that we make it for them to be successful and to move up, the better our organization will be. In the end, they are going to be able to give you something back—they're going to give you loyalty, and they're going to give you the best that they've got because they are thankful for your help.

People always say to me, "Hey, wait a minute Chris, you're giving all this information to people and you are making them better at leadership…What if they take what you have given them and leave? Another lesson learned from John Maxwell is when it comes to growing your employees, he says, "I'd rather invest and grow my people, giving them what they need to be successful and risk having them leave, then not investing in their development and them be mediocre and stay." When you invest in people to get the very best out of them, when you help them achieve their goals, this makes them great. When they become great, they help our organization become great.

Create a Positive Environment

- Make work better
- Give opportunities to grow
- Eliminate stress

As a leader, it is important to realize that you can't motivate people, they have to motivate themselves. But, you can create an environment where they can reach their goals. Our job as leaders is to get the very best out of the members of our team. When you focus on sharing opportunities, growing and valuing people while truly showing you care about them, you develop a positive working environment. This eliminates stress and increases morale.

RULE SIX

Stop Listening to What Employees Are Saying

"The ear of the leader must ring with the voices of the people."

— Woodrow Wilson

Be Aware of Your Employee's Feelings

S top listening to what employees are saying and instead, be more aware of your employee's feelings. In rule 1, we talked about emotional intelligence. One of the five components of emotional intelligence is empathy. I remember back when I was a member of the workforce there were times when my leaders did not listen to my ideas, or I didn't have the right equipment to do my job. I remember what it was like to have poor leadership and thinking that, when my time to be a leader came, I would do a better job. In reality, I didn't start out doing a better job than the poor manager's I'd remembered from my own past. I was worse!

It wasn't until the realization that I wasn't giving my workforce, what they needed to be successful that I changed. I had to start over and actually learn how to be an active listener. Just because you are listening to the words spoken, doesn't mean that you're really, actively listening to the message.

Empathize

You need to take into account both the words and the non-verbal messages that are being sent when someone is communicating with you. Identify the feelings and the emotions that are coming through during the active listening process. Being aware of other people's emotions is very, very important when you are talking with somebody. Make sure that you are able to take their emotions into account. Also, be sure to maintain eye contact.

Don't be afraid to ask others for their opinions. This will make them feel valued. There may be times you need to bring in a third party to help mediate during times of challenge. You may not be able to get an employee to understand your point or you may not understand the gravity of their situation. This is where a third party can assist in lending some assistance to the situation.

Use Humor

Hearing is not listening, just because you are listening to the words that are being said does not mean that real communication, or a meeting of the minds is happening. Sometimes, to achieve communication, you need to be able to use humor. Tough situations broken up with a little bit of humor can really make a big difference in how people feel about the situation.

In the world of Emergency Medical Services, EMT's and Paramedics see some horrific things on a daily basis. We see people on what could be the worst day of their lives. Whether it is welcoming a new life in the world, or holding the hand of a person taking their last breath. When you work in an environment that has a constant level of stress it is important to be serious, but when appropriate, bringing a little levity may help reduce the stress of the moment. As a leader, understanding when this is appropriate comes from knowing who that employee is, understanding their personality, and feeling comfortable that they would appreciate a bit of levity at this stressful time. A word of caution, humor does not work with everyone, and in every situation. Know when the use of humor is appropriate.

Treating Employees Fairly

One of the ways we fail as leaders is not treating employees fairly. We have to remember, we are being watched by everyone in our organizations. If employees see that you are showing favoritism, and they are being treated differently, this is a surefire way to build resentment with that employee.

Being consistent with everyone in your organization will never give you the tag of being unfair or showing favoritism. Everyone deserves to be treated with respect and as fairly as everyone else in the organization.

When people feel that you are fair, and you treat them with respect, this will work in your favor as well. As a rule of thumb be approachable, stay consistent in your leadership practices and respect everyone you come in contact with.

Improve Communication Skills

- Show appreciation
- Connect with people
- Stay positive
- Watch your tone
- Focus on results
- Listen, Listen, listen
- Notice non-verbal feedback
- Request feedback
- Follow-up

Encourage

Your role as a leader is to be there when employees need to bend your ear. Be appreciative that your people trust you enough to come to you and seek your guidance. They may say, "I need your help or guidance" or they may ask, "How would you deal with this customer complaint?" Regardless of the reason, when someone comes to you, show them your appreciation. This is what helps make a connection between people. Put yourself in their shoes always, be encouraging and show your positive attitude.

Watch Your Tone

When employees seek your council, always watch your tone when responding. Sometimes we are caught up in the day, we can forget how important this meeting is for the employee and we respond in a harsh tone. This can be very damaging to your relationship with that employee. If this occurs, make certain you say you're sorry and let them know it was not personal.

Resolve Conflict

By listening to every word as a person speaks, watching their non-verbal cues, asking questions, and giving appropriate feedback, this will send the message to the speaker that you are interested in what they have to say, and you want to help them.

Your body language shows non-verbally that you are open to listening to what someone is saying to you. Asking questions and making comments essentially communicates the idea that, "I can make this work for you. We can fix this and move forward."

One of the biggest components of resolving conflict is, once the conversation is over, we need to follow up with that employee to make sure that their challenge, or problem was really resolved. Did they get the result they needed to solve their problem? It is important to follow up, and many leaders forget this crucial step.

In a couple days ask that employee if they were able to get resolution. If not, as they update you on their progress, ensure them that you are there for them and you are ready to assist further. If needed be the go between to assist in resolving conflict or meet with other parties. Be the resource that helps them get their issue resolved.

Be an Engaged Listener

Being an engaged listener is another component of improving your communication skills. The person speaking deserves 100% of your attention. You need to watch their body language and look for emotional clues as they speak when you are showing that you are an engaged listener. Make sure you respond to both the words and the non-verbal information they are communicating to you as they speak. That's going to help reinforce the message that you are really listening to them. Don't forget to respond verbally with a "yes" or an "I see" and smile and nod as appropriate. Those indicate without interrupting that they have your full attention.

Psychology teaches us when actively listening we should "try to favor our right ear when we're listening." The reason is, your left brain contains the primary centers for speech and comprehension. Those centers are connected to the right parts of our body.

I also use my posture to show that I'm offering someone my complete attention. I sit up straight. I put my work away.

One of the best practices learned from one of my supervisors was when I would come into his office, he would come from behind the desk and sit with me as I spoke. This was a simple expression of how important my time with him was. It made me realize that my desk is where I do my work, my desk is not where I lead from. It was a great lesson, and one that became part of my leadership toolbox.

It feels more personal. It's comforting to feel that your supervisor really wants to help you. People notice those signals that you are offering them with your actions, the message that they are important enough for you to stop what you're doing and pay full attention.

Maintain a Positive Attitude and Environment

There are times when you can easily tell people are upset and sometimes the office itself, its impression of authority, makes them upset. When this seems the case, one of the things to do is find an alternative place to have this discussion. Walk to the cafeteria for a cup of coffee, or find a sitting area outside of the department. In many cases this change of environment helps ease their tensions.

One of the things we don't do well enough as leaders is, we don't allow people to finish their thoughts. We're always interrupting them in conversations. We've got to stop doing this.

If they're a "talker," let them know in the beginning that if you only have a couple of minutes to talk right then. I might say something like, "I have a meeting in fifteen minutes and if you want to talk with me now for a few minutes, that's fine." Maybe I will ask them to walk with me on way to that meeting. Sometimes you may need to say, let me get back to you later. If that is the decision, make certain you do, in fact, get back to them.

Stop Being Judgmental

One of the challenges for leaders when it comes to listening is a tendency to want to judge people. There are a lot of times we don't know why people are in the situations they're in. Just because we wouldn't put ourselves in their situation or live their lifestyle doesn't mean that we should judge them. If you are one of those leaders that is judgmental with your workforce, you must stop this practice at once. It is not your role to pass judgment on anyone. Try a dose of understanding and respect for your team members.

Provide Feedback Based on What you Hear

Finally, provide feedback based on what you hear. Ask, "Is this what you said?" Paraphrase it back to them. You might say something like, "This is what I understand your feelings to be..." Or, "This is what I understand..."

Make Decisions in a Timely Manner

Another common leadership problem is, we don't get back to employees with our decisions in a timely manner. There are times when it may be necessary to find out some information and get back to an employee. Have you ever gone to someone and they told you they would get back to you and they never did? How did that make you feel? Did you have the same level of respect for that person? When you say to someone, "I'll get back to you" that is something that is your obligation to complete. Make sure your word is stronger than oak.

When it comes to getting back to employees, use your cell phone to keep track of your obligations. Sometimes, I may be on the way to a meeting and an employee grabs me to ask a question. It may be necessary to say, "Let me get back to you" - set an appointment in your phone so you do not forget. Again, failing to get back when you say you will decreases your leadership effectiveness.

Barriers to Effective Communication

- Stress
- Out of control emotions
- Lack of focus
- Inconsistent body language

Stay Calm Under Pressure

In the 1972 movie the "Godfather," the character Michael says, "It's not personal, Sonny it's strictly business." Sometimes individuals are going to come into your office and they are going to be very emotional. Maybe they are angry and want to point a finger at you or the organization. You may become defensive and want to give that attitude right back. This is where remembering the above quote and telling yourself this is not a personal attack. This is just business.

RULE SEVEN

Experience comes from Mistakes and Mistakes Come From a lack of Experience

"Knowledge is knowing that tomato is a fruit, wisdom is not putting it in a fruit salad."

– Bryan O'Driscoll

Remember, the first time you make a mistake, it's a mistake. If you make the same mistake another time, that's a choice. A valuable lesson learned throughout my professional career was that mistakes are a natural part of the living, developing and growing process. From an early age we are conditioned that mistakes are bad and we should never make them. Now that we are in the business world this conditioning has taken on a negative effect causing us to not take chances, not offer our ideas, or not take on extra challenges and responsibilities. This is a very debilitating way to think if success is your ultimate goal.

Making Mistakes is Normal

When you understand that mistakes are a natural part of learning, you see that Rule 7 is vital for gaining professional expertise. Once you can embrace this concept, it gives you a better understanding of your capabilities. Remember, experience comes from mistakes and mistakes come from a lack of experience. There is a great quote from Zig Zigler that says, "Set a goal so big that you cannot achieve it, until you grow into the person who can." This quote embodies this idea.

Stop Endlessly Worrying About Past Mistakes

When we worry about mistakes, it doesn't allow us to gain more experience. It just reinforces that we should not make that mistake again. Mistakes come in different sizes, from the silliest, to the dumb, to the more complex. My most recent mistake was locking my 110-pound Akita, Grace, in my office for a run downtown instead of putting her in her kennel— this was a slight oversight— a minor mistake. But, when you come home and your brand new leather chair has been eaten up whose fault is that? Well, my mistake caused me some valuable experience. Now should I dwell on this or know better the next time?

Put Yourself in Situations Where you can Make Mistakes

Whenever possible put yourself in situations that are new, and know that if you make mistakes this is part of your learning process. Going back to the fear of making mistakes, this fear is what holds people back from stepping outside their comfort zone and trying new things. This is a horrible circle; I coach people that are looking for something new. Maybe a new challenge, or a higher paying job, but it's the uncomfortable feeling of failing or making mistakes that keeps them from venturing out to explore new territory. You cannot find the next level of success if you keep looking for it in the same everyday habits.

Mistakes Teach Self-Confidence

There I said it. Believe it or not, when you have to admit mistakes and head back to the drawing board, this helps build self-confidence. Having to admit your mistake gives you an awareness of where your talents lie and what knowledge has to be developed.

There has been more than a couple times where I've tried to implement a new program, or procedure. On paper it seemed like it would work, in practice it sucked eggs. This caused me to go back to my workforce and admit my error and say, "I'm sorry." This not only helped in developing my confidence, but it reinforced confidence within my workforce that I was human, and like most humans, mistakes are made. This gives employees comfort that your organization is not a one-mistake organization.

Don't Allow Mistakes to Ruin Your Life

We don't have to allow these mistakes to ruin our lives. A lot of times, we hang onto our mistakes like badges of honor. We need to be able to give them back and say, "I'll wait for the movie to come out if that's okay." Your role is not to be a historian and remember the past, your role is to forgive the mistake, get back in the saddle and ride to the next adventure.

Mistakes can Teach us to Accept our Fears

Making mistakes helps to teach us to accept fears. What we learn most is more self-awareness about who we are, and what knowledge needs to be developed or polished. This really comes down to accepting responsibility, admitting and saying sorry for the error. There have been individuals that go to great lengths to hide the mistakes they make, or maybe even take the path to blame others. This is never a good practice; your mistakes are the only thing that is unique to you. Your willingness to accept responsibility for your actions adds to your integrity and reputation.

Handling Mistakes and Failures

Mistakes also allow us to inspire others. When we become a mentor, what we are really doing is we are sharing our experiences and our mistakes.

So, what is the best way to go down the path of handling

mistakes? How do you learn from your mistakes? Let's look at a few elements to accepting this practice.

1. First, admit your mistake and take 100% responsibility. Let's take this one step further. To become a great leader, you not only have to accept your mistakes, but also bear the weight of your team's mistakes as well. Some leaders forget this point and "throw employees under the bus" to avoid attention upon themselves. This act by someone who considers himself or herself a leader, to put it as nicely as possible, is cowardly.

2. Determine through investigation and using a root cause analysis how this mistake occurred. Even if this is a personal error, determine how it happened and what you will do next time to avoid this from occurring again. Once you determine how it happened, make note never to make the same mistake twice. In my case, Grace will not be locked in my office ever again.

3. Keep moving forward. Regardless of what has happened with past mistakes hold your chest and head high and move forward as fearlessly as possible. Let's take a page from professional athletes, when a quarterback throws an interception or a pitcher gives up a homerun, they take the ball on the next snap as if nothing ever happened. That's what you have to do. Don't get stuck living in that moment of fear.

4. Mistakes are a moment in time and do not define your whole career. The mistake isn't falling down; the mistake is not getting back up. You need to keep your eye on the big picture, and what is the end result. The end result is for you to move from an apprentice to a journeyman to somebody who is master of their skills. The only way you are going to get there is if you develop from those mistakes.

5. Don't let mistakes ruin your self-confidence. This is another negative habit. When some people make a mistake they continually relive that mistake and allow it to effect their

self-confidence. You need to get out from behind your mistakes and continue to succeed. A mistake within a mistake is when you create failure from the fear of failing again.

While we are on the subject of self-confidence, let's spend a few minutes defining the two main components of self-confidence. They are self-esteem and self-efficacy. Self-esteem is how we see or feel about our own abilities, or ourselves, whereas self-efficacy is our actual abilities.

To boost self-confidence, you have stop listening to that little voice in your head. It seems anytime we step out of our comfort zone to try to do something new, that voice is there to say, "No, you can't do that! Remember, you failed the last time you did that. We can't get outside of our comfort zone, that's going to scare us." That negative self-talk originates from your sub-conscious. The talk you are hearing in your head is what you taught your sub-conscious about yourself. The only way to control this negative self-talk is to think and believe positive thoughts. This is the only way to turn that inner voice into your cheerleader. Ask yourself this question: How much damage does your negative self-talk cause you?

Now imagine if that inner voice was positive with the same intensity. What things would you be able to accomplish?

The F Word: Failure

Have you ever used the F-word? No not that one, I'm talking about the word failure. The F word is the worst word that we use in our professional and personal life. When mistakes are made do you consider it a failure?

If so, you have to change your thought process on the word failure because failure isn't that boogeyman word, it's not that "Nightmare on Elm Street" word—failure is part of living, failure is part of life. Stop giving the word failure the power over you. It's time to learn from your mistakes and move forward. Forgive yourself, and whatever it is you have done in the past, know that it's shaped you into the person that you are today. We've all made mistakes.

Right now, today, it's time to forgive yourselves. More mistakes are going to come as you venture outside your comfort zone. If you allow guilt to build, you're going to be carrying that weight around for years, and it is going to affect your self-confidence and your self-esteem.

Going back to our analogy of how professional athletes deal with failure. Michael Jordan is one of the greatest basketball players of all time. I'm inspired how he approaches failure, he said, "I have missed more than 9000 shots in my career. I have lost almost 300 games. On 26 occasions I have been trusted to take the game winning shot and I have missed. I have failed over and over again in my life and that is why I succeed." When you're feeling challenged, look at one of the greatest basketball players of all time and how he looks at failure, we should not be any different.

Mistakes are part of living, developing and growing. We're taught at an early age that when we make mistakes, this is a bad thing. Because of this, as adults, we have a fear of failure. This holds us back from taking risks. We don't want to take on new responsibilities in case we fail. Once in the workforce, we don't want to make mistakes. Or, we think we have to hide them or cover them up, when we do make mistakes.

Making Mistakes is Normal

Making mistakes is going to be part of who you are as a professional. If we can embrace that, it gives us a better understanding of what we are capable of and allows us to take chances and learn new things. There is a quote by Zig Ziglar that I love, "Set a goal so big that you can't achieve it until you grow into the person who can." At its heart, that quote is about embracing and learning from our mistakes.

Put Yourself in Situations Where you can Make Mistakes

I recommend putting yourself in situations where you make mistakes. It's those mistakes that are challenging and give you confidence when you are able to learn from and overcome them. Big problems make me use a whole host of my skills to solve them.

Mistakes can Teach us Self-Confidence

Having the self-confidence to admit that you made a mistake is also very important. I have a friend who says, "When you fail, get in front of your workforce and fail gloriously!" Let them know that this is an environment where everybody fails and that it's okay.

Mistakes Teach us to Clarify What we Want and What we Don't Want

Learning from your mistakes is very important because mistakes will teach us how to clarify what we want and what we don't want out of life. They help us clarify how we go about doing our job or how we will approach it differently the next time. Mistakes teach us that we have to accept ourselves. We're flawed, but we're also unique and talented. We don't have to allow mistakes to ruin our lives.

Mistakes can Teach us to Accept our Fears

Mistakes teach us to accept our fears. Mistakes teach us about ourselves and how to tell the truth. To say, "I was responsible, that was my mistake. I won't do that again. I'm sorry if that affected the team." That willingness to accept responsibility for your actions gives you a lot of integrity.

Inspire Others with Your Mistakes and how you Handle Failure

Believe it or not, mistakes also allow us to inspire others. When we become a mentor, we share our experiences and mistakes. How do you learn from your mistakes? The first thing that you need to do is take 100% responsibility. It's not about pointing fingers, it's about fixing the mistake. If it is your mistake, stand up and fail gloriously. Take 100% responsibility. You may have to accept consequences but that's part of the solution to the problem. However, if you're committing mistakes on a daily basis, we may have to work within your professional development to help you understand why that's occurring.

What was the Cause of the Mistake?

Find out, what was the cause of the mistake? Get to the root of it and realize why it happened. Ask yourself, was this an error in your process? Was this an error because you were stressed out? Find out exactly why it happened, and if you know why it happened, that understanding will allow you to move forward.

Don't let Your Mistakes Define you

Mistakes don't define you. When I make a mistake, I tend to beat myself up about it, but I learned later on that I wasn't being productive when I was doing that. When you make a mistake, it's OK feel bad about it, but don't let that equate to who you are as a person.

People often hold on to mistakes and they think because of that, they are failures. Growth starts with those mistakes. You learn to be a better professional and a better person from your mistakes. As you are growing and learning, there is room for improvement, we are human and we are going to make mistakes. But, we need to be able to move forward from those experiences.

Negative People

Be sure to stay away from negativity and people that are always negative. We want to only have positive thoughts. Is the glass half full? You're darn right it's half full and when it's empty I'm going to fill it up again!

This is the time to evaluate who's in your life. We have to break ourselves away from negative people and help them become positive. If they're not going to be positive, we may have to end our professional relationship.

How we Handle Ourselves

We need to take good care of ourselves. When we're depressed, when we have low self-confidence, we forget that **we** are the most important person in our lives. We have to do things for ourselves.

Never Give up, Never Accept Failure

There is a solution to everything that we have to do. Never throw that towel in. Be the person that's going to say, "I don't care what that little voice is saying, I'm going to prove them wrong. That little voice, at the end of the day, is you. You need to be able to make yourself more positive. Low self-confidence is horrible and we need to be able to end it. We need to be able to move forward and move our success forward.

We also need to think about our self-esteem and how to improve it. Our self-esteem really deals with the self-worth or our sense of our personal value to ourselves and in the world. In part, this is a personality trait, but again when we have low self-confidence, when we think we aren't going to be successful, we don't think we can be valuable to the team, we don't think we can be valuable to our peers, we have to change that in order to become successful and leader others.

Low self-esteem is one of those contributing factors to saying "I'm not going to try something new." You have to be able to change your mindset. You're not unworthy. You're not incapable. You're not incompetent. In fact, you're a hero. You're a unique person and you need to allow your special gifts that you have inside you to shine.

So how do you know if you have low self-esteem? If you don't have a positive outlook on life, you don't have a positive outlook when you talk to people, you have a perfectionist attitude.

Self-Confidence = Self-Efficacy Plus Self-Esteem

The two main attributes of self-confidence are self-efficacy and self-esteem. Self-esteem is how we view ourselves. However, we have a tendency to blame other people. A blaming behaviors might be thinking, "The reason I'm in this position today is because of my boss. I got fired because I was late four times. If he didn't fire me, then I would still be able to pay my mortgage."

Let's not point fingers, let's fix the problems. Increase your self-esteem. Be positive and let that self-talk be your cheerleader. Imagine how much damage negative self-talk does to you—can you imagine if that inner voice was positive and the things that you would be able to accomplish? You control that voice!

Get Regular Exercise

If you're struggling with low self-esteem, you also need regular exercise. Regular exercise gives you energy, it fends off depression and it makes you feel good about yourself. If there are things that you don't like about yourself or your life, you're the only one that has the ability to change it. No one else can change it for you.

Take Care of Yourself

Take care of yourself. Take care of your needs. And, learn to let the little things go. In rule number 2, we talked about not wasting time and energy on things that you can't control. If we allow those things to weigh us down, it's this big anvil that's swinging over our head and we're waiting for the rope to break.

Remember, you are who you are, and own who you are. Be proud of who you are and those accomplishments are going to come. If you can do that, you're going to be able to build your resume of success.

RULE EIGHT

Motivate and Inspire

"Our chief want is someone who will inspire us to be what we know we could be."

— *Ralph Waldo Emerson*

One of the questions I'm asked most often deals with how to inspire and motivate the workforce. Leadership is about bringing the very best out of our employees. When employees are happy, they are engaged, thus increasing employee satisfaction and productivity, which now equals an excellent customer experience.

With the mistakes and arrogance displayed in my earlier career, I learned a little secret far too late to help. I'm going to share that secret with you right now. To be seen as a successful leader, it is not the work that you do that makes you successful, it's the work your employees do that makes you successful. If your workforce is unhappy, resentful, and disengaged, how well will they be doing their work? So the brass tacks: your role as a leader is to motivate and inspire your workforce to be the very best that they can be. Your reputation and success hinges on this fact.

If I can inspire you, and I could motivate you, there's no bounds to where you can get to. Break out of your current state of awareness, what you *think* your potential is and reach out for opportunity.

One time, I had 350 people in my charge that I was responsible for and I thought it was a lot, but, when you stand in the front the room giving a leadership talk as a motivational speaker, there are thousands of people in the audience! It wasn't until someone inspired me and motivated me to believe in myself that I started seeking bigger speaking engagements. I said to myself, you know what Chris, "You could be a lot bigger than what you think you can be."

Motivation is the powerhouse that drives people to outstanding performance. One of the first things we need to develop is a culture and environment that removes the barriers keeping employees from being inspired. This may include changing your current practice of leadership. If you have a workforce with poor employee satisfaction you need to change your leadership style. You will see the environment change drastically if you practice a leadership style focused on helping your employees. After having a leadership style that people can relate to, next you have to lead by example to set the standards and expectations.

Engage Your Workforce

When we set the standards and model the way we want our teams to treat each other, this projects a clear path for accountability. Work on engaging your workforce. An engaged workforce is a productive workforce. Before you are able to engage your workforce, you have to ask yourself one honest question. Do you value people? Very simply, you will not be able to motivate and inspire people if you do not value their contributions. This will only lead to manipulation, and that's not leadership.

You Can't Motivate Anyone

Here is a fun fact: as you read about the secret ingredients of motivation and inspiration there is one thing you need to know. You cannot motivate anyone. Motivation comes from within each individual.

There are internal and external factors that motivate people. To intrinsically motive your workforce, you need to meet the following needs:

- Make Their Role Significant – individuals need to feel their responsibilities are significant and are of value to others.

- The big Picture – individuals are more successful when they know how what they do fits into the big picture of the organization.

- Give More Responsibility – As you look to inspire and motivate your team, share new responsibilities, which will allow them to experience and grow different skills.

- Always Show Respect – This really speaks for itself.

- Give Recognition and Feedback – Everyone likes a good pat on the back. Begin this step right away.

- Be Fair and Non-Biased – Always be consistent and fair to everyone. The feeling of favoritism destroys motivation.

As a leader your role is to develop a workplace that fosters this ability for motivation to flourish. After the workplace is ripe for motivation to grow, you now have to engage in getting to know your employees. This will give you the needed information on what exactly motivates them.

Creating an environment that allows motivation to grow begins and ends with you. Here are a few suggestions to help you begin this process:

1. Create Future Leaders – When you take an active interest in growing your people, this strikes the match of motivation.

There are people in our departments today that will become very successful in their future. Help them grow, develop experience and set them on the course for leadership success. We will discuss Growing Leaders in Rule 9.

2. Provide a Safety net for Making Mistakes – We all make mistakes, we learned in Rule 7 that mistakes grow experience. When employees know that they are encouraged to think outside the box and if mistakes that occur they will be used as teaching moments, there is a collective sigh of relief. No one likes getting in trouble, and to know you don't run a one-mistake organization give comfort. Now, the first time a mistake is made it's a mistake, the second time the mistake is made it's a choice. That comes with a whole different discussion.

3. Become a Role Model – Why did you become a leader? Was it because of the parking space and the expense account? Were you attracted by more money, or being able to wear a shirt and tie to work? If that was your motivation, these secret ingredients will not help you. Most people get into leadership because they know they can make a difference for their employees. If that was your case, it is essential you becoming a role model and mentor. We will discuss Mentorship in Rule 10.

4. Empower Your Workforce – In today's business world the word power is seen as a dirty word. There are leaders that use power to fuel an autocratic style of leadership. This style of leadership is based on bullying and intimation. When power is used in a positive way, this is the foundation for good leadership. When you share your authority and Empower your workforce to make decisions, complete a project, or lead others this generates a high level of motivation for employees.

5. Teach Conflict Resolution – One important skill members of your organization need to know is conflict resolution. In the everyday business world conflict arises in all different

shapes and sizes. Having the tools necessary to deal with conflict is a necessity for every toolbox. As these challenges arise, being able to determine a conflict even before it happens because you're watching and understanding emotions of the people that are in your leadership team and workforce is a key attribute of a successful leader.

Develop Critical Thinking Skills

- Don't take anything for granted
- Consider the motive
- Do your research
- Ask questions
- Do not assume you are correct
- Break it down
- Keep it simple

Critical Thinking Skills

In everything we do, we need to be critical thinkers. One of the lessons that we learn while building our social skills and conflict resolution ability is that not everybody wins all the time. People must learn how to compromise. Being consistent and being fair are key as you're building your conflict resolution skills. Knowing how to resolve conflict and when to compromise are two cornerstones of critical thinking.

Communication Skills

Building your communication skills is another cornerstone of improving our ability to be critical thinkers. Determine how you communicate, praise your employees, coach them. Everyone wants to be noticed for a job well done. Give them the pat on the back, tell them you know what they've done, right or wrong. We need to be able to coach them and grow them, polish their skills, and eventually help them get to the next level.

Develop Critical Thinking Skills

Critical thinking really comes from breaking down and being analytical about a situation. If there is a problem, use a process. First, ask, do we have to fix it? Do we have to polish it? Do we even have to do anything about it?

Critical thinking involves being able to question and evaluate information. Don't take anything at face value. We need to be able to ask the questions. We need to know why. Not only why, but we need to be able to know the "what," the "how," the "when," the "who" and the "what-ifs" too.

Cultivate an Environment of Motivation

If there is one thing that zaps motivation quickly it's when employees get frustrated and annoyed about not having the answer to their questions. Usually when a member of our workforce has a problem they meet with their supervisor share the problem and ask for a solution. This may have been a good in past business models, but in today's fast paced business world, it is more of a resource to everyone involved if we can develop solid Critical thinking and problem solving skills. Instead of giving solutions, give the parameters for available resources, ask more questions, and help the employee come up with their own solution. This now gives them the tools to deal with similar situations as they arise.

This practice and skill now assists in developing confidence, ownership and the ability to feel trusted into the success of the organization. When you assist in developing Critical Thinking Skills and empower employees to make necessary decisions this shows you believe in the strength of that employee in meeting organizational goals. This in itself is a great footing for encouraging motivation.

Don't Accept Face Value

One of the hard lessons taught to me was never to take things on face value. There are three sides to every story there is your side, my side, and somewhere in the middle is **The Truth**. On occasions, in my career I've made decision based on misinformation and manipulation as well. Teaching your future leaders to question information that is presented is a good practice. This helps to gather, analyze and see all different sides and perspectives

Motive

An additional consideration is to consider the motive. Teach your mentees to ask more questions. Consider why did this issue occur? Who needs to be talked to? Are there other processes getting in the way? If yes then what is it? Getting to the bottom line to figure out why this hurdle is occurring will teach the mentee to get to the root cause of issues. This is a valuable part of critical thinking skill development.

You Might not Always be Right

Nothing hurts employee motivation then a leader that may not be right. It is true leaders make mistakes too. Knowing this keeps leaders and their egos in check.

A favorite story comes from my earlier in my career. There was a Sargent in the Air Force that was not necessarily a fan favorite. After watching us do some work he came to us and said, "I've been watching you do this task and here's a new process I feel is going to work better for you." He continued, "Put this into place right away start immediately." Well in short, this process was horrible, it added steps and took almost twice as long to complete. We went to talk to this Sargent and he was not swayed by our concerns. Members of the team eventually went to talk to the Chief Master Sargent (CMS) about this issue. After sharing our concerns he asked, "Why did you agree to this change?" We said, "We didn't agree to it! The Sergeant just came and said, "Here it is, do it."

The CMS said, "Well, follow me." We went into that Sergeant's office and the CMS said, "Rearrange his office furniture anyway you'd like." We went ahead and put his desk upside down and hung his chair from the ceiling, and moved everything around. When the Sergeant eventually came back to his office, the CMS said, "We thought that this would work better for you and we want you to use your office this way immediately."

The moral of the story was, don't assume that you're right just because you're their leader. Get the people involved who actually do the work and ask them for their opinions. Leaders should never change processes or procedures without the input of the team that does the work.

Developing critical thinking skills is not rocket science, but some leaders have the tendency to turn it into rocket science.

Being an Effective Leader

- Be focused
- Be passionate
- Be assertive
- Be decisive
- Empower employees
- Be confident
- Communicate
- Be self-aware
- Stay humble
- Be honest

RULE NINE

Grow Leaders

"When you are made a leader, you aren't given a crown, you are given the responsibility to bring out the best in others."

– Jack Walsh

How to Create Leaders

- Give Them What They Need
- Be Respectful
- Don't Micromanage
- Lead by Example
- Be Personable
- Stress Vision and Goals
- Do What You see
- Be Decisive
- Show Emotions
- Push the Limits
- Admit When You Don't Have the Answer
- Don't Impose Fear
- Develop Future Leaders

- Encourage Personal Growth
- Help Overcome Weakness
- Hold Folks Accountable
- Ask Questions
- Demonstrate Knowledge
- Be Flexible
- Understand Your Purpose
- Welcome Involvement
- Get to Know Your Team
- Be Transparent
- Hold Brainstorming Sessions
- Be Accessible

Develop Leaders Early

It takes time to learn the skills needed to become a successful leader. It is our responsibility to grow and get the very best out of the people who join our organization, these are the future leaders that will be guiding tomorrow's generation. It is imperative that we develop a process for succession planning as we prepare for tomorrow's business practices. We need to ensure that if we move on to a different organization or retire, the organization itself is going to be maintained. I say to my leadership team, "Stop hiring employees. Instead, hire future leaders." I want them to look each applicant's potential to lead, not just whether or not they can do the technical requirements of the job.

As leaders, it's our role to ensure that we grow the leaders of tomorrow. If we look at motivation from the point of view of a worker, they want to know that the organization and the leadership team are going to invest in their future. As you grow their skills, knowledge and experience, you now multiply your leadership effectiveness, which grows a strong successful organization.

During the time that I've been a leader, I've made it a point to help future leaders. Those leaders have since taken my system of leadership and they've made it their own. They've polished and made it work for them. Those same people have become a mentor to their own future leaders now. As you write your leadership autobiography developing future leaders is part of your career's legacy.

Prepare for the Future Starting now

I often ask people in my organization, "What are your goals?" Maybe they say, "In the next 5 years, I want to be a Supervisor." I'd ask them, "What are you going to do now to become a Supervisor in 5 years?" This question makes people stop and think about how they use their time. If you wait 5 years and then say, "Now I want to be a Supervisor" and it takes another 2 years to get ready for that, you've just wasted 60 months.

I ask them, "Why don't you take a leadership class a month to prepare yourself to become a Supervisor in the future?" This is why it is so important to develop the next generation of leaders early. When they start preparing for this long-term goal now, our organization gets the benefit of these new skills today. You are now able to give added responsibilities, delegate more, and grow that leader of tomorrow.

Educate and Train Employees

You need to be able to educate and train your employees on what leadership is all about. I try to give everyone as much leadership training as they want. Then they begin to understand the science of leadership. This allows employees to understand why decisions, processes and practices are developed. This is also a major part of transparency. Your workforce will never have to wonder why, because they will appreciate how plans become practice.

If you just make decisions in a vacuum and people don't understand why, then there is going to be a challenge. For example, if you are able to explain to them that "the budget is not sustaining for us to buy this piece of equipment," and follow up by giving them the reasons why, then you're teaching them about leadership through your example.

Challenge Employees

Personally, I like to challenge employees. I like to push them out of the nest and make them stretch for things that they may not be able to attain right away. I'm often in the position of believing in them before they believe in themselves. That's what is going to give them the confidence to go to the next level. You are giving them the opportunity to be successful and the support they need to persevere while they learn the skills to get there.

Let Them Interact with Other Leaders

As a student growing up in NYC there were some classes that just did not have my interest. Needless to say, my performance in that class was not the very best it could be. There was also a perception by a couple teachers that my association with the "wrong crowd" was hindering my future development. One of my teachers actually said to me "you will never amount to anything in your life." That was some very interesting psychology from someone that should have been a mentor. There are leaders today that use those same demotivating tactics on their workforce. This is a practice that has no place in the business world.

Luckily, there were strong leaders who believed in me and invested in developing my professional skills in the years after that teacher said I wouldn't amount to anything. They challenged me to believe in me, and said I would become more than what I was at that time.

One of the practices used with my young leaders was to take them to meetings with me as a learning opportunity. This would allow them the opportunity to see what goes on behind that closed door. Employees always seem to ask that question "I wonder what they are talking about in there?" When they are included, it prepares them for the eventuality of being in their own future leadership meetings.

Teach Them to Network

As leaders, we also need to teach our mentees how to network. I used to take my leadership team to conferences and I would always ask them before the day started, "How many business cards do you have?" They'd have a handful, maybe 20 or 30. Then I'd say to them, "You need to give them all away to the people you meet and talk to at this conference. Be sure that you get 20 or 30 cards back and use them to follow up with every person you meet to develop your network. When you get back, send emails to these people and say, 'It was really great meeting you. I would really like to put you in my professional network, will that be okay?' " For however many cards they had, they'd be developing that many new connections.

Provide Support for Employees

Another way to motivate people is to give them different areas of responsibility. If you are able to take your leaders and give them experiences in the different areas of responsibilities within your department, now you are growing their ability to understand the whole operation.

Rotate Employee Positions

It is important that employees learn about what is going on in different departments. Not only will this help develop individuals learning new areas of your organization, most times these new sets of eyes can help that new department with a different perspective based on their experience.

Empower Employees to Make Decisions

Empower employees to make decisions and to guide other people in the department. When they become mentors to other people, they can learn a lot about leadership from that experience. Part of the leadership team's responsibility is to inspire and motivate the workforce so by giving people your empowerment and authority, and giving them the opportunities to use that, they will grow their leadership experience. That's a very big responsibility and they learn how to lead from the ground up.

Develop Mastermind Groups

Mastermind groups bring like-minded people together to discuss, debate and develop together. This weekly meeting could be used as a springboard to hypothetical scenario problem solving, discussing reading assignments, and learning from peer experiences. This type of group begins building the importance of networking and relying on people who want what you want. Working together on a common goal builds teamwork skills as well.

Lunch and Leadership

As a Consultant, conducting this type of leadership training this is one of my most favorite things to do. Whether conducting it live or via online training, several organizations have had me speak with their aspiring and current leaders on different leadership topics on a monthly basis. My discussions are usually coordinated with the department head and developed custom to that specific organization's leadership development needs.

Conduct Leadership Assessments

Leadership assessments are also great resources for developing leaders. You can gather so many data points about strengths and weaknesses, personality types, and learning styles. With this information, goals and individual performance improvement plans can be developed custom to meeting individual needs. There are many great tools out there for you to consider.

The 30,000-Foot View

One of the big differences from being a worker and becoming a leader is the view from which everything is seen. Whereas a member of the workforce is seeing things from ground level, leaders are seeing things from the macroscopic level. It is this big picture perspective that needs to be cultivated and understood as your workforce grows.

Frequent Feedback Sessions

Another important component in growing future leaders is to introduce frequent coaching and feedback sessions. This will allow you the chance to discuss successes, challenges and answer questions. Even when you take an active role in professional development, you cannot assume everything is moving along without hurdles. Regular feedback sessions are paramount to ensure everything is proceeding in a positive direction, at the pace you've set.

RULE TEN

Be a Mentor

"If it's lonely at the top, you are not doing something right."

– John Maxwell

What is Mentoring?

Mentoring is defined as:

1. A trusted counselor or guide

2. A tutor, or a coach

3. An influential senior sponsor or supporter

Key Guidelines for Mentors

- Prepare for mentoring

- Establish the mentor relationship

- Work with your mentee

Mentoring

nitially, there were always people in my career who I looked up to and it seemed that no matter what their role in the company, they always seemed to have an answer to any challenge that popped up. I remember thinking this was a magical process, it seemed that these mentors had this magic bag of tricks where they could access the needed answers and solutions. It was like a mental filing cabinet that served them as their reference for whatever happened next.

I didn't understand how those people were able to be so decisive and calm in fearful times while I was struggling in those areas. Those are the people that I wanted to emulate. I wanted to have their knowledge, their ability to communicate and to articulate their ideas so clearly and powerfully. In essence, I wanted to be like them.

Even as my experience grew, I still recall the first time someone mentioned to me that I was their mentor. It was a bit embarrassing, humbling, and a scary all at the same time. Initially, I remember chuckling a bit, because it took me off guard. This person was coming to me and saying "I've been watching you work, you seem to have all the answers, you have everyone's respect, and I wish to be a professional just like you."

That was when I realized that many people on my teams and in my company are watching me because I'm in a position of authority and leadership—they are trying to better themselves and I'm influencing that. This was a big lesson for me. Here I am handling my daily responsibilities, being watched along the way. This made me think and be thankful I never took shortcuts, or cut corners, I never treated a customer with disrespect, because if I had that might have been the negative path they followed me down. The lesson here is you are always in the spotlight and everyone is always watching.

My good friend and mentor has a great saying, "Always consider as you leave the house, its Act 1, Scene 1 and Action!" It's true, we have to be able to ensure that as we are moving forward in our day, we keep in mind that people are watching us, they want to be like us, and we have to give them the best that we've got.

Establish the Mentor Relationship

I have coaching and mentoring clients that I assist from all different fields—not just the medical field—from small business executives to CEOs. While working at Christian Hospital EMS there was one mentoring experience that truly gave me pride and joy: watching my mentee's development unfold. As a practice, when possible I enjoy adding people to my leadership team with little experience, to teach, grow and mentor them. This allows me the opportunity to teach them how to be great leaders. This one individual was so new, they made countless mistakes while gaining experience.

At one point my boss came to me and said, "I'm not sure this person is going to work out in this role, we should cut our losses now and let them go." My response was, "Give me a little bit of time to shape and help them grow."

Well, fast forward a couple years later, my boss came up to me and said of my mentee, "You made a really great choice picking her for this position." This was a very satisfying feeling to not only be recognized by your workforce as being a great leader, but by your boss who now knows that you have a magic bag of tricks to grow future leaders.

Work With Your Mentee

I've shared that story with that particular mentee a couple times. Jokingly tongue in cheek, "You should not even be working here..." But then the pat on the back sharing how they made themselves successful and a well-respected member of the organization leadership team. Now, I have the honor of watching her pass off the knowledge I shared with her, with her own mentee. This is an extreme feeling of satisfaction.

Keys to Successful Mentoring

- Develop trust
- Define roles and responsibilities
- Establish goals
- Collaborate to solve problems

Developing the Mentor-Mentee Relationship Based on Trust

When beginning a mentor-mentee relationship, first, you need to be able to develop that relationship based on a foundation of trust. The person that is coming to you, your mentee, they need to know that you are going to work in their best interests. They want to know that you are not going to guide them in the wrong direction. I have seen some of my peers guide people in the wrong direction. That's not a relationship based on trust.

As their mentor it is your responsibility to be able to give both the good news and the bad, to share both constructive and corrective feedback, all while growing your mentee's strengths and polishing their weaknesses. Maybe, you are being asked how you would handle a specific situation, or they are asking you for career advice, in the case of being a great mentor never give them the final answer, allow them to make the final decision.

My first leadership role in the military was initially an exciting time. Remembering one of my first leadership meetings, I remember feeling like not having to sit at the kiddie table any longer. That first meeting there was a problem that needed to be addressed and I made the comment to the Chief Master Sargent leading the meeting, I said "Chief, I think we should try this as a solution" for dramatic effect of this story, let's say he slammed his hand on the table and said, "You know Sargent, I have tried that a hundred times and it has not worked." I felt about 2 inches tall. The Chief then followed up with, "But who is to say it does not work the hundred and first time, give it a go." I can tell you that it didn't work the hundred and first time, but he didn't stop my creativity in trying to solve problem.

Think back to Edison with the light bulb, there were 9,999 times that he didn't create the light bulb. Someone said, "How is it to fail 9,999 times?" Edison replied, "I didn't fail, I just showed you 9,999 ways how not to do it."

Define Roles and Responsibilities

You will also need to be sure to define roles and responsibilities in a mentoring relationship. We need to be able to say, "This is how this relationship is going to be, what my role would be, what your role would be." Taking responsibility for somebody's career path is a pretty big challenge. Establishing clear roles is important. You need to have a conversation about the relationship before it begins explaining, "If I'm going to guide you, you need to be able to make changes, and you need to be able to be responsible for your actions." Then you need to determine what types of mentoring would be most effective for that person. Is it that you are going to give them some personal guidance? Are you going to give them some reading to do? How is it going to work for them?

One of the questions he asked me often is: What is the difference between coaching and mentoring? We will discuss this more later on in the chapter. But for now, coaching is more short term and deals with learning a skill, or working on a new piece of equipment. Whereas, mentoring is based on the long term, and deals with overall professional development. In the mentor, mentee relationship it is paramount you help the mentee outline both long and short term goals for growth. Learning how they interact with people and learning how they react in different types of situations is also really important for you to help them develop into that next level of leadership ability.

Offer Timely Constructive Feedback, When it Will Make a Difference

Timing is also important, we need to ensure that as we talk to our mentees, we do it at a time that's crucial for that feedback. An example would be if you saw something that needed to be discussed, and waited 10 days to get around to giving feedback. This lapse of time could have ingrained that practice with your mentee over countless times. This may also make the mentee frustrated and defensive. Ensure all feedback is given as timely as practical. Another tool in your arsenal is develop a style that allows you to give both constructive and corrective feedback. No one likes to be given negative feedback about their performance, but this type of feedback is a vital step in developing high quality performance.

Collaborate to Solve Problems

In rule number 3 we discussed, "there are no problems, just solutions," as a mentor, we need to teach our mentee different ways to solve problems and implement solutions. To be a good mentor, you need to be able to teach people different ways of solving their problems while using their critical thinking and problem solving skills. This would be a great time for you as the mentor to share what experiences you've learned throughout your career.

Often in business and in leadership roles, processes of improvement—just because you are comfortable (or uncomfortable) using a particular process (Six Sigma, Lean), doesn't mean that someone else is not going to find the Six Sigma or Lean Process helpful or useful in their own career. A best practice will be to teach your mentee different types of process improvement strategies. Even if you have settled on one specific strategy in your career, introduce different strategies for them to choose the best improvement strategy for that particular problem.

Mentor vs. Mentee

In my leadership consultant career, I've had some real hard discussions with individuals that refuse to mentor their folks. They worry that after they teach, develop and grow their mentee, that mentee will just leap frog over them and become better than the mentor was. In a nutshell, that should be your hope. As you help in developing people, your goal should not be to create them into a clone of you. Your experiences should guide them, they should polish your teachings and grow them into their own recipe for their ultimate success. What you have to remember, with each and every person you help get to the next step, you are writing the story of your leadership legacy.

Qualities of a Good Mentor

- Willingness to share skills, knowledge
- and experience
- Demonstrate positive attitude
- Be a positive role model
- Take a personal interest
- Exhibit enthusiasm
- Value ongoing learning and growth
- Provide guidance and constructive feedback
- Set and meet ongoing personal and
- professional goals
- Value people

Be Willing to Share Skills, Knowledge and Your Expertise

There are 10 qualities that define being a good mentor. The first is, your willingness to share skills, knowledge and your expertise. Your experience as a leader is ongoing and if you are growth minded you are always learning and improving. Mentoring others doesn't take away anything from you, it adds to your legacy as a leader capable of growing the next generation of leaders.

Don't be Goal Oriented, be Growth Oriented

John Maxwell says—"Don't be goal oriented. When the goal is over, what do you do? You need to be growth oriented instead, to ensure that your knowledge continues to grow throughout your professional career." What's important about being a good mentor is you need to have willingness to ensure that you are sharing what you have learned, you are sharing your knowledge, you are sharing your experience, and you are sharing your skills. The way that you would handle a situation today should not be the way you handled it 20 years ago!

Demonstrate a Positive Attitude and be a Role Model

Always demonstrate a positive attitude, even when things are bad. When we talk about crises in my line of work, there is never a "bad" day. In the face of adversity, you are going to be the one your workforce looks to for answers, guidance, and comfort.

In the first couple of hours, when the Ferguson, MO crisis was growing into the international powder keg it was, I was on the scene trying to get the lay of the land, and making decisions in the face of the protests that were looming. Standing in a group of employees with my mind going a thousand miles a minute, I realized that everyone was looking at me for answers. One of my staff said, "I am scared and this is outside of my comfort zone."

In the face of this challenge, my response was positive, comforting and strong with confidence. My assurance that everything would be okay gave a moment of relief. In the face of adversity, it is you that sets the standards and expectations for others to follow. This is where you stack points onto your leadership reputation and others will want to emulate you.

Take Personal Interest in the Mentoring Relationship

Take personal interest in your mentoring relationship. There is no better feeling than watching someone that you mentored, now becoming a mentor themselves, leading their own organization, or speaking at international conferences to a 1000 people. These are things that you helped people develop into. Again, more chapters into your leadership legacy.

Exhibit Enthusiasm

Part of those accomplishments is that you have grown other

leaders. Your role as a mentor is to always be positive, and to show enthusiasm about your career field. With that said, how are you advancing within your career field? What is your plan to develop your expertise and become recognized? Are you publishing articles, are you speaking at conferences? When you become an expert in your field, this makes the mentor mentee relationship more attractive.

Value Continuing Education

Be sure to value continuing education. We need to think about: How do we become the best that we can be? How do we learn from our mistakes? How do we learn what's going on? We've got to be able to have conceptualization, we've got to be able to have good foresight and we've got to be able to have good vision. To grow as leaders, you need to value continuing education for yourself and others.

Show Tact When Offering Constructive or Corrective Feedback

There will be times that giving negative feedback about a project outcome, or flaw in personality that is not going to be received very well. This type of feedback is hard to hear, but this is where your tact and communication skills will help you. You need to be able to give people constructive and corrective feedback in a way that they are going to be able to accept it.

A lot of this skill comes down to having tact, we've got to be able to give a good feedback, and a little bit of bad feedback, and come back on top of that with good feedback. You might say, "You had some challenges when you were going through this process, you have done a really good job in the past, and I really admire that you handle stressful situations well. But I want to talk about how you handled this meeting, you got a little bit fired up, and you showed your emotions a little bit, so keep that in mind, the next time you are in that kind of situation. But I have to tell you, I'm sure this is the last time that we'll need to talk about it, I really think you are going to do it differently next time." What you are doing there is you are sandwiching what's good about people, you are throwing in a little bit of bad, and then you are putting some good on top of that.

The way you did it Isn't the Only way

You need to remember that, as a mentor, the way you did it, doesn't necessarily mean it's the way your mentee is going to do it, and it doesn't necessarily mean it's wrong if they do it differently. You need to be able to give them autonomy to take your guidance and do what they want to do with it. But remember this is not a personal thing, this is just based on how your mentee wishes to proceed. I have been in mentor mentee relationships where the mentee did not appreciate my guidance, and went against all common sense. It would have been easy to just "kick them to the curb" instead I just bided my time until they came back saying, "I'm ready to learn now." It's not personal, it's strictly business.

Treat Your Mentee how You'd Like to be Treated

If you are a mentor, it's important to think about how we'd want to be treated, how we'd want to be talked to if we were the mentee in the relationship. Maybe we were talked to pretty horribly in our career, but that doesn't mean that we have to be like that to somebody else. The mentor mentee relationship is built on a foundation of trust and respect. These have to be the attributes that develop this relationship.

Set Goals

One of the most important steps in developing a mentee is assisting them in not only setting goals, but reaching them as well. If you can assist this process, you will see growth and development in this relationship. One step that is a must is holding your mentee accountable to following their plan of achieving goals.

Value Your Mentee's Opinions

Within this relationship, there may be the time where the mentee wants to try something you know may not work. Are you going to be the mentor that says, "I've tried that 100 times and it hasn't worked?" Or, are you going to be the one who says, "Who is to say it does not work the 101st time, give it a shot." Remember that 101st time may be the answer no one else was able to find. It's important to value people, and also value their opinions, and what they bring to the team.

5 Differences Between Mentoring and Coaching

There are five differences between coaching and mentoring and you need to understand them in order to decide when it is appropriate to choose one vs. the other.

Differences Between Coaching and Mentoring

- Coaching is task orientated
- Mentoring is relationship orientated
- Coaching is short term
- Mentoring is long term
- Coaching is performance driven
- Mentoring is development driven
- Coaching does not require design
- Mentoring requires a design phase

Coaching is Task-Oriented

Coaching is task-oriented, while mentoring is relationship-oriented. That doesn't mean that when you have a mentee you are not going to be able to coach them, there may be times that you are coaching somebody that you are not taking under your wing as a mentor.

When you think about coaching being task-oriented, it focuses specifically on specific tasks that people are responsible for completing. As a coach, when evaluating their performance, if you see issues try to classify them into one of these four reasons:

- They were not trained correctly
- They do not have the proper equipment
- to do their job
- It's something in the environment or that is
- around them that is causing problems
- It's just a behavioral issue

When you are able to determine that cause of the challenge, this makes coaching much easier. Say it's a conflict resolution matter or they're worried about how their communication skills will come across in a stressful situation. This is your opportunity to coach and guide development.

Mentoring is Relationship-Oriented

Mentoring is about building a relationship. Mentoring is about building and maintaining a long-term relationship. You follow up with your mentee, teach them more from a personal perspective based on your own experiences as a leader, learn about them over time, set specific goals and develop different components of their leadership skills.

Coaching is Short-Term, Mentoring can be Long-Term

Coaching is short-term. Maybe you are teaching a new computer system to an employee, it might take a few weeks and then the coaching is no longer needed. In contrast, mentoring is a long-term relationship. I have people who consider me to be their mentor that I still talk to and we haven't worked together for the past 10 years. They read my articles online, they are able to see what I am doing in my career field, and they call me to brainstorm how to handle situations that come up in their career.

Coaching Focuses on Improving the Individual Performance, Mentoring is Development Driven

In coaching, you want to improve the individual's performance of a task or tasks. When you are in a coaching role, it's specifically performance driven. You want to be able to get very best out of them and help them correct any challenges they are facing.

In contrast, mentoring is development driven. You are not worried about the task, you are worried about the person. You might focus on teaching them how to handle conflict resolution or improve their communication skills.

Coaching can be Impromptu, Mentoring Requires a Plan or Strategy for Development

Coaching can be done during a spare moments. You could be walking past somebody and notice that they are not doing a skill the correct way, and you decide to go over and engage them with some coaching. You might ask, "Is this the way you have always done it? Is this the way you were taught to do it?" This will give you an understanding of how the employee was taught to complete this skill. Often, you can coach somebody in 30 minutes just walking past their office and saying something. It has no real design.

In contrast, mentoring requires planning and follows a development process. When developing a plan for a mentee, my process is to sit down for a discussion together we develop a plan for moving forward. This is usually a written plan with objectives and goals that outlines how we will be moving forward. This acts as our blueprint. There may be times where you have to deviate from that plan as situation's dictate. For this reason, make certain your plan is a living document that allows for change.

Coaching is Usually With Your Direct Manager, Mentoring can be any Person Helping to Develop an Individual

A big difference between coaching and mentoring is that coaching often deals with the immediate manager of the department. Whereas, with a mentor it could be somebody that is not even in your department or even in totally different career field.

When to Consider Coaching

- When there are new procedures and
- processes to implement
- When the company is going to expand
- When there are new skills to be learned

When to Consider Coaching

When should we consider coaching? When you as an organization are ready to teach the employees specific components of a skill or task. You need to ask yourself: Is there a new process? Is there a new procedure? Is there a new tool that needs to be implemented? That's a good time to consider coaching.

When There are new Procedures and Processes to Implement

Sometimes employees in an organization aren't meeting the expectations. In the medical field it is vital that all procedures are followed to the letter. We would monitor treatments, management and care delivered to patients. One of our best practices allowed us to grade employees based on system and national averages. An example would be starting an IV. Even though every patient is different and starting IV's can be challenging, all Paramedics had to maintain a 90% success rate in IV placement. If individuals fell below the system average, this was cause for a discussion and a possible performance improvement plan. Being able to ensure your workforce is meeting expectations ensures that outcomes are as high as possible.

When the Company is Going to Expand

Hopefully your company will be ready for some expansion. When this occurs, you may have to add more people and conduct coaching and training on a greater scale. This would be a great time to include incumbent employees in the training of their peers.

When There are new Skills to be Learned

Are there new skills that need to be learned, or new process to put into place? That is a good time to implement coaching. In today's work environment there are new processes and pieces of equipment that are needed all the time. If you are bringing those into your organization, it's going to be best to using coaching to teach those new skills. One of the things that you think about in those situations is: if you know you are going to be getting those new pieces of equipment months from now, start your training as soon as you can, and make it an ongoing training process so that when the equipment comes in 4 months, you've already taken advantage of that time frame to be prepared for the change.

When to Consider Mentoring

- When developing leaders for succession planning
- Developing diversity to decreases barriers
- toward success
- When wanting to develop better work-life
- balance in the workforce

When to Consider Mentoring

It is best to consider mentoring when your company is looking to develop new leaders. One of the things that we did in our organization is, we said: "Don't hire workers, hire future leaders." We also need to take responsibility for teaching new hires to be leaders. We need to make sure that they are paired with somebody, or that the mentee chooses somebody that they want to emulate and work with from the very beginning of their time with the company.

Succession Planning

In our present day there are 10,000 baby boomers retiring every day. This will last for the next 2 decades. Knowing this, how are you planning on developing a succession plan for your future organization? We can look at succession planning for those who are going to be retiring in the next 5 years and begin that process with asking them to become mentors to the next generation of leaders in order to preserve some of their knowledge and experience and pass it on to the new employees.

Developing Work-Life Balance in the Workforce

Finally, we need to be able to develop a workforce that balances the professional and the personal aspects of life. Sometimes we find people who will be the first ones at their desks and the last ones there, and they are coming in on Saturdays and are always answering their phones. One of the lessons a mentor needs to teach their mentee is to develop a positive work life balance.

As a mentor, you may be a workaholic and spend all your time at the office. This has become a good practice for you, but this should not be the practice you pass along to your mentee. In my family, I have 4 beautiful, smart, funny children, with each their own personalities (they paid me to write that). A couple of my kids, have kids of their own. The reason I share this story is, my kids are grown and have lives of their own now. So, I can spend more time focused on my career assisting organizations in developing into the very best they can become.

I travel for days on end, spend hours a day in the office, and make the most of the twilight of my career. When you are guiding and growing a mentee, you have to remember that they have families, young children, and even though they wish to emulate you, you have to teach them to strike the balance between watching their kids grow, and how to develop a line item budget. That budget will be there tomorrow, but their son hitting his first homerun happens today. Help them balance work and life. It's a valuable lesson.

CONCLUSION

Ultimate Leadership: The 10 Rules of Success has given you a valuable set of leadership tools to guide you into growing into the best leader possible. Becoming a good leader is a process and a practice, it isn't something that you learn only from a book. You must be willing to look inside yourself and identify your own strengths and weaknesses as a leader and then actively practice improving on your weaknesses and playing to your strengths. Keep yourself in your talent area as much as possible and delegate certain tasks to those better suited for them whenever it makes sense.

Don't be afraid to make mistakes as you learn, but make smart mistakes, put safety measures into place and as they say, "Fail faster." Reading this book, seeking to grow and improve your leadership skills is just one way to "fail faster." The more you fail, the more you learn. The more you learn and gain valuable experience and insights, the better leader you will become.

Failing, and making mistakes taught me some valuable lessons leading to me having the skills to build an award-winning organization. If you want to engage your workforce, increase employee satisfaction thus increasing productivity which leads to an awesome customer experience, follow these 10 rules.

—*Chris Cebollero*

If you are interested in teaching Ultimate Leadership 10 Rules for Success, you can purchase the license at http://www.chriscebollero.com on our products page.

ABOUT THE AUTHOR

Chris Cebollero is an internationally recognized leader, author and motivational speaker. Chris spent 30 years in the medical field where he led hundreds of medical professionals. He has a proven track record of developing the next generation of leaders.

In 2014, his experience served him and his Emergency Medical Service teams well as they were thrust right in the middle of the riots, looting and assaults during the Ferguson crisis in Ferguson, MO.

Chris is currently the Senior Partner of Cebollero & Associates, a leadership/medical consulting firm. Chris is also a certified member of the John Maxwell Team.

Join us for other great leadership development opportunities. Visit the leadership and coaching website http://www.chriscebollero.com where you can find other great leadership development topics.

Chris is available for one on one or group coaching, organizational leadership development and leadership training.

Join us for the Ultimate Leadership podcast on our Products page where we have great discussions with thought leaders on leadership philosophy. Chris is available for coaching in person or via telecommunication.

If Chris can assist with your leadership development objectives please feel free to contact him at (314) 297-6850 or cebollero@gmail.com.

For More Information

For more information or to connect with Chris visit his LinkedIn page at:

https://www.linkedin.com/in/chris-cebollero-leadership-consultant-2940bb33.

Or, visit his website at: http://www.chriscebollero.com.

54249854R00064

Made in the USA
San Bernardino, CA
11 October 2017